The New Supervisor's Handbook

Julian Talbot

"A leader is a dealer in hope."

- Napoleon Bonaparte

Table of Contents

About This Handbook vii

Leadership 1
   Principles of Leadership 1
   What Is Leadership? 2
   What Type of Leader Are You? 3
   Leadership Myths 7
   Traits of a Leader 12

Communication 21
   Communication Styles 22
   The Art of Active Listening 26
   Non-Verbal Communication 31
   Team Meetings 38
   Team Briefings 39
   Brainstorming and Facilitation 40

Health, Safety, and Environment (HSE) 43

Time Management 47

Management Systems 49
Management Policies 53

Decision Making and Problem Solving 59
The Eightfold Path of Problem Solving 61
Root Causes and the Ishikawa Diagram 73

Performance Management 77
Motivation 77
Intrinsic and Extrinsic Motivation 78
Counseling and Discipline 79
General Notes 80
Conducting Counseling or Discipline Interviews 83

Report Writing 89

Gaining Experience 93

Some Final Thoughts 97

Appendix: Recommended Reading 101

A Corporate Tool 103

About This Handbook

"Effective leadership is not about making speeches or being liked; leadership is defined by results not attributes."

Peter Drucker

I wrote this book for new managers and supervisors. It's basically a short list of some of the things I wish someone had told me when I got my first promotion.

Being a first-time supervisor is a scary thing. It's great, but it's daunting, complex, and uncertain. There seem to be so many more ways to mess up than to do things right. After three decades of management experience and hard-won lessons, I've tried to distill a few key lessons I came across in those early days. A boss of mine once told a friend, "At least Julian never makes the same mistake twice." I'm pretty sure that's not true, but I think my friend's reply summed me up when she responded: "So he's pretty creative, then?" Indeed, I seem to have made so many mistakes along the way that I must have invented a few new ones. In hindsight, that's probably a good thing. It didn't always feel like a good thing, however—that is, until one day I came across the simple truth: The secret to success is to fail more often.

~ School of Hard Knocks ~

Experience is a rough and long road.

When asked for a formula for success, Thomas John Watson, Sr., the founder of IBM, stated, "It's quite simple, really. Double your rate of failure. You are thinking of failure as the enemy of success. But it isn't at all. You can be discouraged by failure or you can learn from it. So go ahead and make mistakes. Make all you can. Because remember, that's where you will find success."

Shorter Path

Failing more often is definitely a path to success, but it's not the only one. Indeed, you can travel a much shorter path if someone gives you a map of the terrain and a survival guide. That's where this book comes in. It's not overly long or complex. I've tried to stay away from management theory and academic ideas on leadership. This is a book for the first-time supervisor and it is designed to help you bypass a few of the traps I've made for myself and then fallen into. You'll no doubt create your own traps, but when you do, hopefully you'll find something in here to help you fashion a rope and haul your way out of the mess.

Traps

I can remember someone sending me some tips on counseling employees, just after I'd made a complete hash of a counseling interview. I thought, "If only my friend had sent this to me *last* week…." With the benefit of hindsight, activities like learning, gaining experience, counseling, and a hundred others are easy. I don't even know what I was worried about. But as my friend pointed out, I'm creative, so I'm perpetually learning from yesterday's mistake.

One of the lessons I learned was that by investing a bit of time to learn from the experience of others, I can spare myself some headaches. And hopefully you will, too.

The workplace today is a constantly evolving environment, and assuming the role of leader is a challenging and rewarding experience. You will find yourself supervising staff who have varying levels of experience and motivation. Even if you have many years of management experience, you will still find a few useful pointers in here—if only to help the supervisors who report to you.

As a supervisor and leader, you have only two basic responsibilities: achieving the organization's objectives and ensuring the welfare of the people who report to you. I have compiled this handbook to provide you with guidance and some tools that can help you with the day-to-day supervision of your staff. In this book, you will find that I use the terms "supervisor" and "manager" interchangeably.

It is my hope that this book, apart from shedding some light on frequent mistakes and saving you the worry about them, will also encourage you to develop your leadership skills. I urge you to seek out further resources and training in leadership. It is one of the most challenging of professional disciplines to master, and there's always something more to learn!

I wish you the best of luck on what is likely to be one of the most rewarding journeys you will undertake—helping others reach their full potential.

Julian Talbot, 2014

2 Basic Responsibilities

1) Achieving the org's goals.

2) Ensuring the welfare of the people who report to you.

Leadership

"Go to the people. Learn from them. Live with them. Start with what they know. Build with what they have. The best of leaders when the job is done, when the task is accomplished, the people will say we have done it ourselves."

- Lao Tzu

Principles of Leadership

"I suppose leadership at one time meant muscles; but today it means getting along with people."

- Mahatma Gandhi

The essence of leadership is accomplishing things through other people. Much has been written on the topic of leadership; indeed, it is a complex field worthy of lifelong study. If I had to give you my top tips in a single list, the list would read as follows. I think you could benefit from simply embracing the following principles:

1. Be a role model.
2. Be yourself.
3. Practice active listening.
4. Praise effectively.
5. State clear expectations.

6. Know yourself and seek self-improvement.
7. Be technically and tactically proficient.
8. Develop a sense of responsibility among your staff.
9. Make sound and timely decisions.
10. Know your staff and look out for their welfare.
11. Keep your team informed.
12. Seek responsibility, and take responsibility for your actions.
13. Ensure that assigned tasks are understood, supervised, and accomplished.
14. Train your staff as a team.

What Is Leadership?

"Leadership: The art of getting someone else to do something you want done because he wants to do it."

- Dwight D. Eisenhower

Leadership is the actions by one or more persons that influence (guide) the behavior of one or more persons in a group setting. These actions by the leader and/or the group are often intentional in that they are meant to influence, or to change, the behavior of other people. The actions must be successful, at least in part, if they are to be regarded as the results of the leadership. Attempts to change behavior that do not result in any changes are exactly what they sound like: unsuccessful attempts at leadership. The psychologist Martin Chelmers defined leadership as "a process of social influence in which one person can enlist the aid and support of others in the accomplishment of a common task."

Leadership does not follow a specific style or process. The style or type of leadership that is effective in one situation may not work very well in another. There are dozens of effective styles and types of leaders. Furthermore, there is no one style that is universally effective. However, and as we will discuss later, good communication skills are essential for *all* types of leadership.

Many types of leadership, especially long-term or political leadership, require the ability to separate personalities from issues. People associate issues with personalities. Many people carry grudges against others from former clashes, and understandably this interferes with any hopes of collaborating together in the future. It is often necessary to separate friendship roles from leadership roles. In many positions, such as on committees and project teams, you may be cooperating with another member on one issue and opposing him on another issue, perhaps at the same time. This requires keeping personality and profession separate from one another; in other words, these issues should not become personal. Granted, this is a most difficult endeavor, especially for inexperienced managers. The attainment of such a skill—one that is not actively pursued (nor always needed) by many—requires considerable practice. The saying "Don't take the argument out of the room" is very difficult for many people to achieve, but it becomes easier over time and with practice.

What Type of Leader Are You?

"It is better to lead from behind and to put others in front, especially when you celebrate victory when nice things occur. You take the front line when there is danger. Then people will appreciate your leadership."

- Nelson Mandela

Everyone has her own style of leadership, and above all, it is important to *be yourself*. Be authentic! There are a number of behaviors we can all learn from to improve our leadership skills. Among these are the three most basic styles of leadership:

➢ Autocratic (authoritarian) leadership

➢ Democratic (participative) leadership

➢ Laissez-faire (delegative) leadership

Each style has its own strengths and weaknesses, but they all share a very significant commonality: their flexibility. Remember that the underlying principle behind being a good leader is the concept of *situational leadership*. In other words, different situations call for different leadership styles. Every wise leader knows this. In an emergency such as a military engagement or a catastrophe, when there is little or no time to come to agreement and when a designated authority has significantly more experience or expertise than the rest of the team, an autocratic leadership style may be most effective. Among a highly motivated and aligned team with a homogeneous level of expertise, however, a more democratic or laissez-faire style may be best. The style adopted should be the one that most effectively achieves the objectives of that particular group while balancing the interests of its individual members.

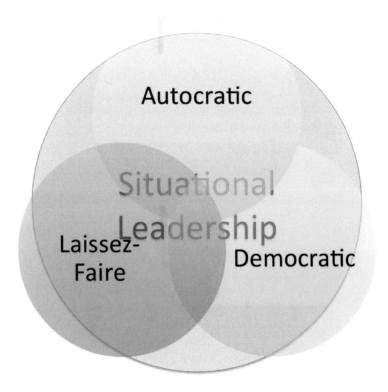

Figure 1: Leadership styles

The effective leader manages to use all three styles of leadership when and where appropriate, without ever going to extremes with any particular style.

Autocratic (Authoritarian) Style

Under autocratic leadership, all decision-making powers are centralized with the leader; a dictatorship is one such example. These leaders do not entertain any suggestions or initiatives from subordinates. The autocratic management style, also called the *authoritarian style*, provides strong motivation to the manager and permits quick decision making because only one person decides for the whole group and can keep each decision to himself until feeling the need to share with the rest of the group.

This is often considered the classical approach. It is one in which the manager retains as much power and decision-making authority as possible. The manager does not consult employees, nor are they allowed to provide any input. Employees are expected to obey orders without receiving any explanations. The driving force of motivation is produced by creating a structured set of rewards and punishments.

This leadership style can be extremely effective if used judiciously and at appropriate times. Most staff, however, do not respond well to this management style, particularly if it's used excessively. But again, autocratic leadership is not all bad. At certain times, such as in the types of situations below, it is the most effective style to use.

➢ There is limited time in which to make a decision (e.g., emergency response or military engagements).

➢ Untrained employees do not know which tasks to perform or which procedures to follow.

➢ Employees do not respond to any other leadership style. (This is a rare situation).

➢ There are high-volume production needs on a daily basis.

➢ Another employee challenges a manager's power.

The autocratic leadership style is likely to be counterproductive in situations in which the staff can reasonably expect to have their opinions heard, decision making requires input from subject-matter experts (e.g., when complex problems need to be solved), or when morale is low and turnover and absenteeism are high.

Participative (Democratic) Style

The democratic leadership style encourages the leader to share her decision-making abilities with group members by promoting the interests of the group members and by practicing social equality. The democratic leadership style is also called the *participative style,* as it welcomes employees as a part of the decision-making process. The democratic manager keeps his employees informed about everything that affects their work and shares decision-making and problem-solving responsibilities. Moreover, this style requires the leader to be a coach who has the final say but gathers information from staff members before making a decision.

Democratic leadership can produce high-quality and high-quantity work for long periods of time. Many employees like the trust they receive, and they tend to respond with cooperation, team spirit, and high morale. Typically, the democratic leader develops plans to help employees evaluate their own performance and encourages them to establish goals.

Like the other styles, the democratic style is not always appropriate. It is most successful in the following situations:

➢ Employees are highly skilled or experienced.

➢ Operational changes must be implemented.

➢ A manager must resolve individual or group problems.

As a general rule, this style of leadership is the most productive in the modern workplace. It's particularly effective in situations in which you want staff to participate in decision-making and problem-solving duties, when you want to provide opportunities for people to develop a high sense of personal growth and job satisfaction, and when changes have to be made or problems solved that directly affect employees. It's also the right approach when you have a large or complex problem (such as a safety issue) that requires significant input from a range of subject-matter experts.

Democratic leadership should not be used when there isn't enough time to get everyone's input, when staff may have a conflict of interest (voting on their own pay raises, for instance), or if the team simply doesn't have the necessary expertise.

Laissez-Faire (Delegative) Style

A person may be in a leadership position without providing leadership, basically leaving the group to fend for itself. Subordinates are given a free hand in deciding their own policies and methods. Laissez-faire leadership, also known as *delegative leadership*, is a type of leadership style in which leaders are hands-off and allow group members to make the decisions. Researchers have found that this is the style that generally leads to the lowest productivity among group members. Laissez-faire leadership is characterized by very little guidance from leaders, complete freedom for the team to make decisions, and situations in which team members are expected to solve problems on their own.

Nevertheless, laissez-faire leadership can be effective in situations in which group members are highly skilled, motivated, and capable of working on their own. While the term for this style implies a completely hands-off approach, many leaders still remain open and available to group members for consultation and feedback.

Laissez-faire leadership is not ideal in situations in which group members lack the knowledge or experience they need to complete tasks and make decisions. Some people are not good at setting their own deadlines, managing their own projects, or solving problems on their own. In such situations, projects can run off-track and deadlines might be missed when team members do not receive enough guidance or feedback from their leader.

Leadership Myths

"Management is doing things right; leadership is doing the right things."

- Peter Drucker

Leadership, although largely talked about, has been described as one of the least understood concepts across all cultures and civilizations. Over the years, many researchers have stressed the prevalence of this misunderstanding, stating that the existence of several flawed assumptions, or myths, concerning leadership often interferes with individuals' conceptions of what leadership is all about.

Myth 1: Leaders are egotistical.

No, not necessarily. Real leaders don't need to lead 100 percent of the time. They are able to contribute and accept the leadership of others. Not only that; they know the power of relationships, respect, communication, and humility— all key elements in being a successful leader. These are not egotistical attributes.

Myth 2: Leadership is a rare ability.

Given the fact that there are leaders everywhere, it's not as rare an ability as one might think. Without leaders inspiring people to accomplish common goals, little would actually get done in this world. On most teams, every person who participates acts as a leader on occasion within her work group, company, industry, or community, in their own area of expertise whether or not she is acknowledged as such.

Myth 3: The person with the highest title is the leader.

Well, that depends on your definition of leadership. If you accept that a large part of leadership is in one's ability to influence his own response to situations, that person can be in any role and any position to do that. It's not the sole reserve of the senior management team.

Real leaders are acknowledged by their peers, supervisors, and subordinates. It's not a matter of one's position within an organization. It's a matter of who has the best skills, knowledge, and resources to enable the team to achieve a particular shared goal.

Myth 4: Leaders only give orders.

While a leader may occasionally have to give an order or make a decision in a vacuum, the best leaders inspire rather than order. They do this by building relationships, a procedure that allows them to identify the strengths and weaknesses of the contributors in their organization. Then they use this knowledge to position all contributors in a way that allows them to best succeed so that the group, as a whole, reaches its goal.

In Western cultures, it is generally assumed that group leaders make all the difference when it comes to group influence and overall goal attainment. Although common, this romanticized view of leadership ignores the existence of many other factors that influence group dynamics. For example, group cohesion, communication patterns among members, individual personality traits, group context, and the nature or orientation of the work, as well as behavioral norms and established standards, all influence group functionality in varying capacities. For this reason, it is unwarranted to assume that all leaders are in complete control of their given group's achievements.

Leadership is about the future, not the past. Ralph Waldo Emerson summed it up well when he said, "Our chief want is someone who will inspire us to be what we know we could be." Good leaders gain followers out of respect and their ability to cause people to work toward a particular goal—and the greater that goal, the more inspiring it is. People follow because they can relate to the vision or goal personalized by the leader. A good leader helps people become better than they are. A good leader creates a work environment that attracts, keeps, and motivates its workforce.

Myth 5: Leaders are extroverts.
Leaders aren't all extroverts. There are actually highly successful leaders who are introverts. Half of the leaders whom I've ever known (including my current boss, the successful founder and leader of a seventy million dollar organization) are introverts. The ability to communicate well with a wide variety of people and to be comfortable addressing groups is part of leadership, but many leaders have had to dig deep to discover these abilities within themselves. Bill Gates, Warren Buffet, and Hilary Clinton—just three of the most celebrated leaders of the twenty-first century—are all chronic introverts. And it hasn't stopped them one iota!

Myth 6: Leaders command a following.

Although leadership is certainly a form of power, it is not demarcated by power over people; rather, it is a power *with* people and one that exists as a reciprocal relationship between a leader and his followers. Contrary to popular belief, the use of manipulation, coercion, or domination to influence others is *not* a requirement for leadership. In actuality, individuals who seek group consent and strive to act in the best interests of others have the potential to become exceptionally effective leaders (e.g., class president, court judge).

Real leaders recognize that people aren't waiting eagerly for their next command. There are times when project plans conflict with other events; key people who might need to participate might not be able to; and sometimes there's nothing you can do about it, even as a leader.

Myth 7: Followers exist to support a leader.

The best form of leadership is *servant leadership*, a term often attributed to Robert K. Greenleaf, who is considered the founder of the servant leadership movement. Servant leaders contribute to the well-being of an organization by striving to meet other people's needs. The accomplishments of a team of inspired contributors will always outstrip the accomplishments of teams that are not personally invested in either the goal or their commitment to a leader. When leaders focus on serving the members of their team, treating them as individuals rather than a faceless group, relationships form that are based on loyalty, trust, and respect. It's those relationships that inspire people to "go the extra mile" when a project gets tough because their *hearts* are invested in it, not just their heads.

Myth 8: Leaders are chosen by other people.

The common perception is that leaders are leaders only because other people chose them to be. But in fact, leaders have to first acknowledge the desire to lead. If you don't put yourself out there as a prospective leader, people aren't just going to appoint you as one. Once you step out and offer yourself, people will either confirm or deny your leadership. People don't choose leaders; they acknowledge them.

In fact, there is a school of thought that says leaders are chosen because they convey a message that people believe in and support. Overall, my experience is that others decide if you are a good leader based on their experience of you, but typically leaders are self-appointed. Only you can really decide if you want to be a leader or not.

Myth 9: Leaders are born.

All leaders are born into this world, but they are not necessarily born as leaders. We're all born. What we do with what we have before we die is up to us. According to some, leadership is determined by distinctive characteristics present at birth (e.g., extraversion, intelligence, ingenuity). However, it is important to note that leadership also develops through hard work and careful observation. Thus, effective leadership can result from nature (i.e., innate talents) as well as nurture (i.e., acquired skills).

Few of us remain the person we were when we were born. We are shaped by our surroundings and nurtured by those who raise us. All behavior is learned, including leadership behavior.

Myth 10: All groups have a designated leader.

Despite preconceived notions, not all groups need a designated leader. Groups that are primarily composed of collaborative individuals, are limited in size, are free from stressful decision making, or that exist only for a short period of time (e.g., project teams, casual sporting teams) often undergo a diffusion of responsibility, with leadership tasks and roles being shared among members.

Again, this depends on your definition of leadership. If you believe leadership is the art of bringing out the best in others, why restrict that to work? What about leadership in your relationships with your significant other, your children, and your friends? Leadership is *influence*, and we exert influence all the time on the people with whom we interact. Good leaders do that well to achieve mutually beneficial results.

Group members actually tend to be more contented and productive when they have a leader to guide them. Although individuals filling leadership roles can be a direct source of resentment for followers, most people appreciate the contributions that leaders make to their groups and, consequently, welcome the guidance of a leader.

Traits of a Leader

"An expert is a person who has made all the mistakes that can be made in a particular field."

- Niels Bohr

The equation for success as a leader is very simple: The more leadership traits (tools) you develop, the greater the probability of your success in most types of leadership—and, indeed, in most careers. Below are fourteen traits of effective leaders. The fourteen leader traits + motivation = successful leadership!

1. Personable

An outgoing personality—the ability to enjoy "working the crowd"—is a very useful skill, both in the role of leadership and in many other parts of life. I have a friend who, whenever he is in a meeting or at a party, makes sure that he greets every single person and shakes their hand. Personable people make good leaders, and they are often charismatic, funny, warm, and attentive to others' needs.

What exactly is charisma? The definition of this term is difficult to pinpoint, and it's an overall debatable term. It is commonly thought of as the ability to gain very quickly the attention, respect, and trust of others. Famous leaders like Martin Luther King, Jr., and John F. Kennedy are said to have had great charisma. Indubitably, charisma it is an extremely effective tool for leaders in certain situations, but it is also difficult to learn.

Humor and warmth are effective in most leadership (and non-leadership!) situations. If you are not fortunate enough to have those traits innately, you can develop them. Start by practicing and broadcasting your lovely smile and laugh!

Having a good memory is another useful characteristic—the ability to remember personal characteristics such as names and facts about the other person's family, such as how many children he or she has, etc. People like to hear their names. It shows that you recognize them as unique individuals.

2. Persuasive

Communications skills include oral and written skills. You must be able to speak effectively in public and, in most cases, you must have good writing skills also. The old KISS principle (Keep It Simple, Stupid) is timeless in its utility.

Words are often not enough to persuade someone to take a certain action. Most people today attain most of their information from the Internet, TV, and newspapers, all of which use simple styles with plenty of color, pictures, and graphs to convey ideas. Pictures and other visual aids are especially useful in helping people understand abstract ideas and persuading them to see your point of view.

3. Persistent

Keep trying. Most social changes, large and small, develop gradually (and that's as it should be). Major changes in values and beliefs often take generations to occur and it is unusual for major social changes to occur in less than a few years or even decades. Changes in the educational system often take several decades. If change occurs too fast, people become uncertain about what is right, good, or appropriate. They lose their sense of security. Something as simple as a small change in the curriculum of the local school system may take years. But if the idea is good, the results may last decades and affect many people. Also realize that in a historical perspective, the changes you are working toward may be small and incremental—just a dot on the map at this moment. Yet great things have small beginnings, too. This means that, yes, what we do may seem insignificant (and may very well be, in the grand scheme of things), but it doesn't have to be (and isn't always)....

Be prepared for an effort lasting several years when you begin the process of bringing about change in your organization or community. *Leadership of major projects will require a large amount of stamina and perseverance.*

4. Patient

There are times when you will need to relax and wait for events or time to pass. Many new ideas will become accepted after people have had time to think about them. Most people who are angry or excited about a proposed change will cool down over time. Patience is a hard attribute for many young people (and not-so-young people) to learn. Most changes, especially if they are worthwhile, do not happen quickly. Patience is an essential trait for leadership, as is self-discipline.

Patience and persistence are essential twins for getting things done. Always remember that leadership and change take time. Patience and persistence are very difficult traits to master, especially for the newer generations who are used to more fast-paced lifestyles, cutting-edge technologies, and rapid-fire updates. Modern culture wants things *now*—not tomorrow. But the real world does not work that way. Some changes will occur slowly.

5. Perceptive

As a leader, you must be sensitive to other people's wants and needs, as well as to changes in those wants and needs. Being perceptive to another person's situation often results in securing that person's trust. A gifted politician is one who can always carefully perceive the current mood of his constituents. The ability to listen is an essential skill of a perceptive leader. You must stay in touch with your supporters. If the group is large or unorganized, this will require more effort.

6. Principled

People who are principled are typically honest and trustworthy, two traits that do and will continue to lead the way and save the day. Most people will believe and follow someone whom they trust. Also, because they have nothing to hide, principled people usually communicate with openness and candor—two characteristics that most people appreciate. There are always a few people who will try to take advantage of such traits, unfortunately—but the vast majority of people will appreciate them.

To be principled, follow the ageless Golden Rule: "Do unto others as you would have them do unto you."

7. Praise-Giving

Almost everyone enjoys recognition, especially if she has worked hard to achieve a certain result. You can't say too many kind words, especially if you speak them in a sincere manner. We're not talking about flattery here; this is about genuine appreciation. If you, as a leader, are working with a committee or team, make absolutely sure that you give everyone public recognition. If you don't, you may find it difficult to garner people's support the next time you need help. It's essential, however, that the praise is deserved and that you are specific about why you are praising someone. Too much praise for too little reason detracts from its value and from your credibility. You can quickly develop a reputation as being overly effusive or insincere if your praise isn't appropriate to the context. One caveat, however: It's important to know people's preferences, as some people prefer to avoid being the center of attention and might actually desire to be recognized for their efforts in private, via e-mail, or in a small group setting. As a general rule, however, *praise in public and criticize in private.*

I cannot emphasize it enough: *It is very important to give people recognition for their contributions.* A self-effacing leader who bestows the credit to his supporters will attract many more followers than one who brags on "my" accomplishments. A simple "thank you" is very effective when sincerely given and meant! On the other hand, one mustn't be loath to accept compliments, either; accept them in the same way you give them: graciously, politely, and genuinely.

8. Positive

A leader should always see the future as bright and optimistic. Tomorrow *will* be even better than today! American sociologist W.I. Thomas wrote many years ago about self-fulfilling prophecies. He said that if a person or group believes a thing to be true and operates as though it were true, often it becomes true through their actions. This has been proven often in education and other fields. If a leader takes a positive stance, it will become more popular, and the desired action is more likely to occur. Always assume that someone will closely examine your stance on almost anything you say or do. Pessimism breeds negativity. Optimism breeds opportunity.

9. People-Oriented

Leadership must be of, by, and for the people. The only reason for leadership should be to benefit people. A common tendency is to look for the benefits to an individual, not to the larger group. One reason why many so-called leaders are distrusted today is because they are seen as self-serving, primarily interested in their own benefits. Many people see politics today as a "good old boys' club," with the main players receiving high salaries and super-plush benefits, not at all like the citizen–legislators the founding fathers had in mind. Harry S. Truman summed it up well when he said, "It is amazing what you can accomplish if you do not care who gets the credit."

10. Possibility-Minded

A leader must be realistic when determining what is actually possible. How much can realistically be accomplished within the time and with the resources available? How strong is the desire for change? Determining which ideas in any organization or setting are politically and economically feasible and which are not is a key characteristic of any leader. Do not jump into solving a problem until you have given very careful consideration to defining the problem. Will other people support the proposed solution? A little caution is a good asset for a leader. Bold and swift action by the knight on the white horse occurs primarily in the movies. An old folk saying has considerable wisdom for leadership: "Fools rush in where angels fear to tread." That doesn't mean, however, that you shouldn't take risks. Imagination, daring, and the art of the possible are the hallmarks of leadership. The British Special Air Service motto of "Who Dares Wins" is worth keeping in mind when you are trying to decide on a course of action. Just make sure that you are realistic.

11. Practical

A leader must realize that pleasing all of the people all of the time is not possible. You must be practical when making decisions that cater to the majority, perceptive enough to realize when the majority is right, and strong enough to take action without the support of the majority when the majority is wrong. At the same time, you must be strong enough to stand by your convictions and accept the criticisms—valid and invalid—that are sure to come. 'Practical' and 'possible' are twins that are considerably interrelated.

12. Progressive

An effective leader is a visionary who will move the group forward. Incorporating new ideas, strategies, and concepts of leadership and communication into your personal style is a perpetual function of leadership. Sometimes progress may mean maintaining the current situation, but mostly it involves moving the group (and yourself) further forward.

13. Prepared

A leader must be knowledgeable about her goals, the means for reaching them, and the tools necessary to meet them, as well as about the people in the group. An effective leader must be both organized and prepared. Many a leader has opened their mouth and inserted their foot, only to suddenly find that they was no longer regarded as a leader. In my early days as a junior leader, it sometimes felt that I opened my mouth only to change feet. Get used to making mistakes. Be prepared to admit your errors, apologize, learn from them, and move on with good humor.

14. Power-Building

Even the best leaders can't tackle most leadership jobs alone. They need to have followers and know how to motivate these people to willingly become involved to get the job done. *Power* in this context is more about influence, mutual support, and establishing effective alliances. Colleagues (both leaders and followers) need to trust each other if they are to accomplish something successfully; in turn, leaders must be able to delegate from a position of mutual trust. A correlating trait is the ability to network—to build linkages of friends and acquaintances who may be able to provide needed assistance at some future time. A classic study by James Coleman many years ago showed that *who you know* is one of the most important factors that influences life success.

Close examination of the above traits shows that all of them can be nurtured, learned, and developed. Some are learned early in childhood, while others are learned later on. However, the average person can make major improvements in any of these areas. Personally, I know that many of my characteristics have changed greatly since my early years. If I were the same person as I was then, I could not begin to do what I do today. *Changes in personality are very possible, but only you can make the change for yourself. The very first step is to want to do it.*

Characteristics of Admired Leaders
A survey of 15,000 managers worldwide

1. Honest 87%

2. Forward-looking 71%

3. Inspiring 68%

4. Competent 58%

5. Fair-minded 49%

6. Supportive 46%

7. Broad-minded 41%

8. Intelligent 38%

9. Straightforward 34%

10. Courageous 33%

11. Dependable 32%

12. Cooperative 30%

13. Imaginative 28%

14. Caring 27%

15. Mature 14%

16. Determined 13%

17. Ambitious 10%

18. Loyal 10%

19. Self-controlled 5%

20. Independent 5%

James M. Kouzes and Barry Z. Posner, "What People Surveyed Feel Are the Most Important Traits of Leaders," in Credibility: How Leaders Gain and Lose It, Why People Demand It. (Hoboken, NJ: Jossey-Bass Publishers, 1993), 14.

A survey of 75,000 people in 2002 by the same authors found that little had changed over the ensuing nine years. Four characteristics in this survey received more than 50 percent of the votes:

> ➤ **Honest**—If people are to follow someone willingly, they first want to assure themselves that their leader is worthy of their trust. The vast majority

of people want to know that the person who is leading them is honest, ethical, and principled.

➤ **Forward-looking**—People expect leaders to enunciate a clear vision of a future that is worth striving for. Whether this ability is called a vision, dream, a calling, a goal, or a personal agenda, you need to know where you want to be before you can expect others to join the journey willingly.

➤ **Competent**—We all need to believe that the person who is leading us is competent to do so. You must be demonstrably competent, capable, and effective if you are to bring out the best in others and enable them to act.

➤ **Inspiring**—Leaders are expected to be enthusiastic, energetic, and positive about the future. Inspiring leadership speaks to our need to have meaning and purpose in our lives. Optimism about the future is the essence of being able to breathe life into our dreams and aspirations.

Other qualities the survey respondents admired included intelligence, fair-mindedness, open-mindedness, supportiveness, straightforwardness, dependability, cooperation, and determination.

If this list sounds far too daunting, then perhaps leadership isn't for you. If it sounds challenging but doable, then congratulations, you're on the right path! Leadership is always challenging. And one thing that will help you, above all other characteristics, is to simply stay in good humor and not take yourself too seriously. *A good sense of humor can be a wonderful tool in leadership!*

Communication

"A general is just as good or just as bad as the troops under his command make him."

- General Douglas MacArthur

As a Supervisor, you will need many capabilities, but in the end, your job comes down to just two activities:

➤ Making decisions; and,

➤ Communicating.

Of these two, the ability to communicate well, gets my vote as the single most important ability of a good Supervisor. In fact, one of the single most common criticisms of leaders is the quality and quantity of their communication. There are may aspects to communication however if I had to sum up my advice, it would be to:

➤ Make time to keep your people informed.

➤ Respect the different communication styles of your people.

➤ Pass on any information that may be relevant.

➤ Pass information up the line as well as downstream.

➤ Become a skilled listener!

Communication Styles

" The single biggest problem in communication is the illusion that it has taken place."

- George Bernard Shaw

It is beyond the scope of this book to explain the vast range of different communication styles as this is a topic that you could spend your life time and several PhD's studying, however I would be remiss if I didn't at least provide an overview of communication styles.

If you've ever watched two who have different preferences sometimes have difficulties communicating, almost like they are talking a different language! Have you ever been in a conversation where you knew the other person just wasn't getting your meaning? Or perhaps where the other person just wasn't making sense to you? The simple fact is that we all think slightly differently, process information in our own unique ways and prefer to communicate in our own style. There are several different broad styles of communication. Everyone has elements of all these styles, but most of us are naturally inclined to prefer one or two over the rest.

The most common communication preferences are visual, auditory and kinesthetic (touching, doing or feeling – the latter typically in terms of our emotions) with a fourth communication style known as Auditory Digital. I should add that there are also people who have preferences for interpreting the world via gustatory (taste) or olfactory (smell) senses however this is rare. It isn't very common for these preferences to be dominant in humans and people who are strong in these areas often find careers as chef's, wine tasters, perfume makers and the like. It's statistically unlikely that you work with people who have preferences for olfactory or gustatory communication so we'll focus on the four most common styles.

The 4 styles are Visual, Auditory, Kinesthetic, or Auditory Digital. Essentially, we tend to think in pictures, sounds, feelings, or information.

Visual

People who think visually memorise things by seeing pictures and get less distracted by auditory input. They prefer to send and receive information in a visual format. You can often tell a visual person because when you are talking to them, they will use phrases like: "see what I mean", "it looks like", "at first appearance", "show me", "get the picture?" and will prefer to use visual metaphors. They may have trouble interpreting long verbal instructions (these people prefer face to face meetings over telephone calls or teleconferences) and their mind may wander if you use long verbal communications. They understand things quickly however when they can picture it in their minds.

Auditory

Auditory people love to communicate verbally but may be distracted by outside noises when communicating. They also like to learn by listening to audio books or audio training courses. These people love to communicate via the phone. Tone of voice and words used are also important to an auditory person and they are often musical or at least very interested in music. When you are talking to them, they will often use phrases like: "I hear you", "that sounds good", "I'm all ears", "how does that sound" or "that rings a bell".

Kinesthetic

Kinesthetic people learn best by actually doing a thing or physically practicing it. A strongly kinesthetic person may talk slowly and often doesn't respond well to pictures or verbal instructions. They may not even hear their name called when they are engaged in a task because they are so intensely and physically/emotionally involved in it. Kinesthetic in this context refers both to physically feeling an object and to emotionally feeling something. They usually have strong intuition and make decisions based on gut feeling. People who are strongly kinesthetic often use language like: "that feels about right", "let me get a handle on this now", "let's tap into", or "that idea seems solid".

Auditory Digital

Auditory digital (Ad) people person can be difficult to pick as they often show signs from all the other styles but what's going on inside is quite different. They prefer working with information and data. They learn and communicate by creating or learning steps, systems and procedures. They are very logic driven and often do well in the sciences or computer industry. You can tell an auditory digital person when they say things like: "I'm just processing this", "that makes sense", "if I understand correctly...", "I need some time to consider", "the way I perceive it", or "I know that...".

What's your personal preference?

Reading the above descriptions may remind you of some of your colleagues, friends, family and even yourself. The main thing to remember is that all of us have the ability to use any and all of the communication styles but everyone has one (or sometimes two) preferences. Some people are balanced across all styles and can easily communicate with others in the style that their audience prefers. Most of us however, have to consciously adapt our communication style to reflect the preferences of others.

It's important to remember that no particular style is better or worse – just that some of us will have distinct preferences which drive our typical interactions. In the end however, if you want to communicate with someone effectively you need to mirror their communication preferences. It isn't their responsibility to read your mind and the act of communication is based on what is received – not what is transmitted. You may think you've adequately transmitted your message but never assume. If you're using emails as the basis of your communication, that will work really well with the visual people and to a certain extent with people who prefer Ad as their primary communication style but you will definitely achieve a poor result with the people in your organisation (or family) who have a strong auditory preference.

Practical tips.

Be alert for signs of thinking styles that are different from yours. You'll get cues from the type of words they use. Equally however, when you find yourself getting frustrated in a conversation or over a period of time with a particular person, that's a red flag for you to pause and check how they prefer to communicate. If you get frustrated or cannot communicate with someone that's a flag to notice how they are different from you. To avoid this:

- Consciously listen to work out their preferred style and use the words and concepts from their preferred communication style. Use phrases such as "I see what you mean", "that sounds good", "how do you feel about that?", etc that align with their preferred communication style.
- If they are more visual, draw it out, make pictures or describe how things look. Take the time to prepare and give them a visual model/process or photograph that illustrates what you are saying.
- If they are more kinesthetic, touch them, show them and if possible, engage them in actually doing the activity. At the very least, don't expect them to sit still for too long and don't take offence if they fidget. The more they fidget, the more they are staying alert. Some kinesthetic also like to talk about feelings and if so, they will get much more engaged if you tell them the 'why' of what you are talking about. For example, how you feel when that project comes in on time or how you felt about the last activity, etc.
- If someone is more auditory, tell them on the phone or in person. Strangely enough you would achieve better communication by reading out a memo to them than by just giving it to them as a written document or email. It's a small thing but one that makes a huge difference.
- For people who are more auditory digital, send them a procedure or flowchart, stick to the data and use logical steps. Back up your case with facts and reason.

Communication styles and personality types is a complex subject beyond the scope of this book, but the above should hopefully provide some insights. If you are interested to know more (and as a supervisor, you will need to) I'd suggest that you do some reading on topics such as:

- Neuro-linguistic programming (NLP)
- Myers-Briggs Type Indicator (MBTI)
- DISC personality assessment

The Art of Active Listening

"One of the most sincere forms of respect is actually listening to what another has to say."

- Bryant H. McGill

In the words of Epiticuls, *"We have two ears and one mouth so that we can listen twice as much as we speak."* If all you remember from this section on communication is that you should use them in that ratio, then you will become an excellent communicator.

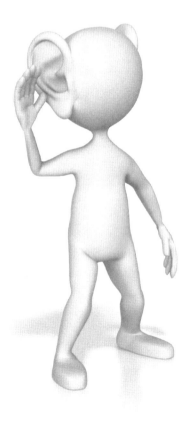

Figure 2: The art of active listening is a core skill

Good listening skills are an essential characteristic of a good leader. As a leader, you must be very aware of the feedback you are receiving from the people around you. If you are not a good listener, your future as a leader will be short. Of course, being a good listener is a skill important in many other settings, too. Active, appreciative, and perceptive listening are guaranteed to enhance your social relationships and interactions of all types, including dating, marriage, parties, work, friendships, and so on.

The definition of good listening skills will vary from one situation to the next. For example, what is effective feedback varies from one person to another; some people you are listening to may need more feedback than others.

The following attributes of good listening are suggestive of the skills needed. There is some overlap among the various attributes, but each suggests something different.

➢ **Concentration.** Good listening is typically hard work. At every moment, we are receiving millions of sensory messages. Nerve endings on your bottom might be telling you that the chair is hard. Others might be indicating that your clothes are binding. Nerve endings in your nose might be picking up the smells of French fries being cooked. Meanwhile, your ears are hearing the buzzing of the computer fan, street sounds, music in the background, or dozens of other sounds. And your emotions are reminding you of that fight you had with your mate last night, while a thousand more signals are knocking at the doors of your senses. And yet at a given moment, you have to repress almost all of these sensory messages and concentrate on the verbal sounds (and visual cues) from one source: the speaker. Most of us have not been thoroughly trained in maintaining this kind of concentration. Over time, however, and with experience and observation, we can drastically improve the art of effective listening.

➢ **Mental focus.** First of all, you have to focus your attention on the words, ideas, and feelings related to the subject. Concentrate on the main ideas or points. Don't let examples or fringe comments detract you. All of this takes a conscious effort.

➢ **Attention.** Attention may be defined as the listener's visual concentration on the speaker. Through eye contact (see below) and other body language cues, you communicate to the speaker that you are paying close attention to his messages. All the while, as you are reading the verbal and nonverbal cues from the speaker, the speaker is reading yours. What messages are you sending out? If you lean forward a little and focus your eyes on the speaker, the message is that you are paying close attention.

➤ **Eye contact.** Good eye contact is essential for several reasons. First, by maintaining eye contact, some of the competing visual inputs are eliminated. Second, most of us have learned to read lips, often unconsciously, and lip reading helps you understand verbal messages. Third, a significant part of many messages is nonverbal; it is by watching the eyes and face of another person that you can pick up clues about the content. Finally, your eye contact with the speaker is your own feedback to this person concerning her message: "Yes, I am listening, I am paying attention. I hear you." A person's face, mouth, eyes, hands, and body all help to communicate to you. No other part of the body is as expressive as the head.

➤ **Receptive body language.** Certain body postures and movements are interpreted with specific meanings in different cultures. (It is worth noting that many nonverbal cues—such as the examples I'll be listing in a moment— vary from culture to culture just as the spoken language does; here I'll be referring to an American context, although, of course, it's not exclusively American.) The crossing of arms and legs is perceived as a closing off of the mind, body, and attention. Vertical nodding of the head is interpreted as agreement or assent. If seated, leaning forward with the upper body communicates that you're paying attention. Standing or seated, maintaining an appropriate distance is important—too close and you might appear to be pushy or aggressive; too far and you might be regarded as cold or detached.

➤ **Understanding of communication symbols.** A good command of the spoken language is essential in good listening. Meaning must be imputed to the words. For common words in the English language, there are numerous meanings. The three-letter word "run" has more than one hundred different uses. As the listener, you must concentrate on the context of the usage to understand the message. The spoken portion of the language is only a fraction of the message. Voice inflection, body language, and other symbols send messages also.

➤ **Openness to the message.** You should be open to the message the other person is sending. It is very difficult to be completely open if only because each of us is strongly biased by the weight of her past experiences. We give meaning to the messages based on society's teachings and on what our parents, teachers, and peers have taught us that the words and symbols mean. Talk to someone from a different culture and watch how they give other meanings to words. Or listen openly and objectively to a person with very different political or religious beliefs than you. Can you do that? Really? It is wonderful if you can, but relatively few people can genuinely listen to, understand, and appreciate messages that are very different from their own. If you cannot, it is time to start practicing; as a leader, you will need to understand a wide range of opinions on often-controversial subjects.

➤ **Restating the message.** Your action of restating the message as part of the feedback you're providing can really enhance the effectiveness of good communication. Insert a comment such as this: "I want to make sure that I have fully understood your message…"before paraphrasing it in your own words. If the communication is not clear, such feedback gives the opportunity for immediate clarification. It is important that you state the message as clearly and objectively as possible.

➤ **Ability to question and clarify.** Questions can serve the same purpose as restating the message. If you are unclear about the intent of the message, ask for more information after allowing sufficient time for explanations. Don't ask questions that will hurt or embarrass the other person or cause him to lose face. Only part of the responsibility is with the speaker. You, too, have an important and active role to play as the listener. If the message does not get through, *two* people have failed: both the speaker and the listener.

➤ **Empathy (not sympathy).** Empathy is "the action of understanding, being aware of, being sensitive to, and vicariously experiencing the feelings, thoughts, and experience of another." Sympathy, on the other hand, is "having common feelings" (*Merriam Webster's Collegiate Dictionary*, 10th edition). In other words, as a good listener, you need to be able to understand the other person, but you do not have to become like her or even agree with her. Simply try to put yourself in the speaker's position so that you can see what she is trying to communicate.

➢ **Strategic pauses.** Pauses can be used very effectively when speaking. For example, pausing at some points while providing feedback can signal that you are carefully considering the message and consciously thinking about what was just said.

➢ **Avoiding interjection.** There is sometimes great temptation for the listener to jump in and say, in essence, "Isn't this really what you meant to say?" This carries the message of "I can say it better than you can," which promptly stifles any further messages from the speaker. Often, this process may degenerate into a game of one-upmanship in which each person tries to outdo the other; obviously, very little valuable communication occurs in this situation.

➢ **Leaving the channel open.** A good listener always leaves open the possibility of additional messages. Your brief question or a nod will often encourage additional communication.

➢ **Refraining from talking.** This is very obvious but very frequently overlooked or ignored. An important question is *why* are you talking? To gain attention for yourself? Or to communicate a message?

We typically hear only what we want to hear and remember only part of what we've heard. Good listening can improve both the content and quality of what we hear and remember.

A good leader is good listener. A good listener may be or may not be a leader. But a good listener is usually a popular person, which is an important step in becoming a leader. People like to be around someone who listens well.

Today is the day to start developing those good listening habits!

Non-Verbal Communication

" What you do speaks so loud that I cannot hear what you say."

- Ralph Waldo Emerson

Every day, we consciously and unconsciously respond to, and transmit, countless nonverbal cues and behaviors including postures, facial expression, pauses, proximity, touch tone of voice, eye gaze, obvious gestures, and microgestures. All of our nonverbal behaviors send strong messages and they don't stop when you stop speaking either. Even when you're silent, you're communicating constantly. It's not my intent to make you an expert in non-verbal communication, but rather to provide some practical guidance and help you realize how important this skill is to a supervisor or leader – indeed to any human being.

So what is nonverbal communication and how to we use it? Essentially, it involves communication through wordless (mostly visual) cues between people. It is often referred to as body language, but nonverbal communication encompasses much more than just signals transmitted by the body. From our handshakes to our eye contact, nonverbal details reveal who we are and impact how we relate to other people. We communicate information in nonverbal ways using clusters of behaviors. For example, someone with crossed arms might simply be cold, a frown could mean they just remembered they had forgotten something on the shopping list, and direct unblinking eye contact might mean they are very interested in what we have to say. Put crossed arms, a frown and unblinking eye contact together at the same time however, and we would be wise to consider the strong possibility that they are indicating disapproval.

The good news is that we already know a lot about nonverbal communications and that you don't need to be an expert. With practice and some conscious attention to others, you can become more accurate in understanding people's communications and in spreading your own message. If you only ever read one book on nonverbal communication but actively applied it, you would already have put yourself into the top ten percent of communicators. The bad news is that reading that book it won't make you a mind reader. Contrary to some articles in popular magazines, even the experts are no better than 80% at predicting if someone is telling the truth.

Luckily, you don't need to be a human lie detector. If you just learn to understand when someone is comfortable or uncomfortable in a particular situation
or with a particular topic you'll be a much more adept communicator. By coming back to a topic repeatedly during a conversation or even over several conver-
sations, you will start to know if it's the topic or some other issue that is making
them uncomfortable. For example, when you ask one of your staff if they have
finished a particular task many people will say "yes" or "almost" even if they
are struggling with it. If you are sensitive to understanding their nonverbal messages, you will quickly be able to tell if "yes" means "yes!" or if it means "er, I
don't want to disappoint you boss by admitting that I'm struggling, but I could
really use some help right now…". If the message is truly the first meaning
(Yes!) then you can move on quickly, but if their body language is transmitting
the latter message, you'd be wise to pause and ask a couple of open-ended questions or offer some assistance.

Why nonverbal communication matters

How you behave, listen, look, move, and react tells other people whether or not
they can trust you. It expresses whether or not you care, if you're being truthful,
and how well you're listening. When your nonverbal signals are congruent and
match up with the words you're saying, they increase trust, clarity, and rapport.
When they don't, they generate tension, distrust, and apprehension.

Quite simply, if what comes out of your mouth and what you communicate
through body language are in conflict, the listener has to choose whether to
believe your verbal or nonverbal message. Most times, they're going to choose
the nonverbal. They do this because unconsciously, they realize that nonverbal
communication is a natural, unconscious language that broadcasts our true feelings and intentions in any given moment.

In fact, no matter how we may try to mask our nonverbal communication, it will
leak out in our body language and nonverbal messages. This is because our subconscious brain and in particular our fight-or-flight reptilian brain will be over-
riding our attempt at deception. Most of us learned early in life to sit a certain
way to convey a certain message, and to not cross our arms, or to shake hands
in a certain way in order to appear confident or assert dominance. The truth is

that such tricks aren't likely to work unless you truly feel confident and in charge. Quite simply, we can't control all of the signals we are constantly sending off about what we are really thinking and feeling. You may be able to mask it for a few minutes with carefully orchestrated body language but the harder and longer you try, the more unnatural your signals are likely to come across.

If you want to become a better communicator, don't just become more sensitive to the nonverbal cues of others, but also to your own. Be congruent and honest, so that you can use your nonverbal communication to reinforce and emphasize your messages. If you're feeling overwhelmed by stress, take time out. Give yourself a moment or at least some deep breaths to calm down before you jump back into the conversation. Once you've regained your emotional equilibrium, you'll be better equipped to deal with the situation in a positive way.

The Elements of Nonverbal Communication
Together, the following nonverbal signals and cues communicate your interest and investment in others.

- Facial expressions are one of the key areas for reading nonverbal communication. Consider for example,how much information can be conveyed with a smile or a frown. While nonverbal communication can vary between cultures, the facial expressions for core emotions such as happiness, sadness, anger, disgust, contempt and fear are similar throughout the world. Many of these expressions pass briefly across the face in a microgesture lasting perhaps $1/30^{th}$ of a second. Experts like Paul Ekman have spent decades deciphering these and developing training courses to help people consciously recognize such microgestures but your subconscious will almost always see them. Without training, you are unlikely to spot them but nonetheless, trust your intuition - if something seems odd it's quite likely that you've subconsciously seen a microgesture of contempt or similar.
- Touch is another key element of nonverbal communications. Think about the messages given by a weak handshake, a warm bear hug, a reassuring slap on the back, a patronizing pat on the head, or a controlling grip on your arm. Touch can be used in many ways: to

communicate affection, familiarity, sympathy, aggression and many other emotions.

- Space. Have you ever felt uncomfortable during a conversation because the other person was standing too close and invading your space? We all have a need for physical space, although that need differs depending on the culture, the situation, and the closeness of the relationship. You can use physical space to communicate many different nonverbal messages, including signals of intimacy and affection, aggression or dominance. The amount of distance we need and the amount of space we perceive as belonging to us is influenced by a number of factors including social norms, situational factors, personality characteristics and level of familiarity. For example, the amount of personal space needed when having a casual conversation with another person usually varies between 18 inches to four feet depending on the individual and their environment. A farmer in central Australia meeting someone from Hong Kong for example, is likely to find the conversation challenging when they both try to adopt their normal spacing requirements.

- Our posture and gestures involve movements and signals which communicate meaning without words. Consider how our perceptions of people are affected by the way they sit, walk, stand up, or hold their head. Common gestures include waving, pointing, and using fingers to indicate numeric amounts. The way you move, stand and carry yourself communicates a wealth of information to the world.

- Paralinguistics refers to vocal communication that is separate from actual language. When we speak, other people "read" our voices in addition to listening to our words. Things they pay attention to include rhythm, speed, volume and pitch, your tone and inflection, and sounds that convey understanding, such as "ahh" and "uh-huh." Think about how someone's tone of voice, for example, can indicate sarcasm, anger, affection, or confidence. Consider the powerful effect that tone of voice can have on the meaning of a sentence. When said in a strong tone of voice, listeners might interpret approval and enthusiasm. The same words said in a hesitant tone of voice might convey disapproval and a lack of interest. Take the following sentence: "I never said she stole the book" and try saying it seven times out loud, with emphasis on a different word each time. You'll quickly see how dramatically meaning can change.

- The visual sense is dominant for most people and eye contact is an accordingly major element of nonverbal communication. The way you look at someone can communicate many things, including interest, affection, hostility, or attraction. Eye contact is also important in maintaining the flow of conversation and for gauging the other person's response. Looking, staring and blinking can also be important nonverbal behaviors. When people encounter people or things that they like, the rate of blinking increases and pupils dilate. Looking at another person can indicate a range of emotions, including hostility, interest and attraction.
- Our choices regarding color, clothing, hairstyles and other factors affecting appearance are also considered a means of nonverbal communication. Appearance can also alter physiological reactions, judgments and interpretations. Just think of all the subtle judgements you quickly make about someone based on his or her appearance. These first impressions are important, which is why experts suggest that job seekers dress appropriately for interviews with potential employers.

How to use nonverbal communication

There are many different types of nonverbal communication and they can play several significant roles that can make your life as a supervisor a lot easier (or a lot harder if you don't understand nonverbal communications):

- Congruence: nonverbal communications can confirm the message the person is making verbally.
- Contradiction: nonverbal messages can contradict a message the individual is trying to convey.
- Correction: nonverbal communications can correct a verbal message. For example, a person's gestures or eye movements can often convey a far more vivid message than their words.
- Confirmation: nonverbal communications can add to or complement a verbal message. A physical gesture such as an arm touch or a pat on the back can emphasis and confirm your message of praise to a staff member and significantly increase the impact of your words.
- Emphasis: nonverbal communications can accent or underline a verbal message. Pounding the table, for example, can send a clear message about the importance of your message that words alone may fail to convey.

Pay attention to inconsistencies between verbal and nonverbal communications. Nonverbal communication should be consistent what is being said and vice versa. Is the person saying one thing, but their body language something else? For example, are they saying "yes" while shaking their head no?

Look at nonverbal communication signals as a cluster of signals and don't read too much into a single gesture or nonverbal cue. Remember, you can't tell if someone is lying so focus on noticing their comfort or discomfort and where it occurs. Consider all of the nonverbal signals from eye contact to tone of voice and gestures. Taken together, are their nonverbal cues consistent—or inconsistent—with what their words are saying? Are they talking politely to you but their eyes keep looking towards the door?

It's important to recognize, though, that it's our nonverbal communication— our facial expressions, gestures, eye contact, posture, and tone of voice—that speak the loudest. The ability to understand and use nonverbal communication, or body language, is a powerful tool that can help you connect with others, express what you really mean, and build better relationships. Once you understand the basics, learning how to manage stress and emotions in the heat of the moment is one of the most important things you can do to improve your nonverbal communication. Stress compromises your ability to communicate. When you're stressed out, you're more likely to misread other people, send confusing or off-putting nonverbal signals, and lapse into unhealthy knee-jerk patterns of behavior. Furthermore, emotions are contagious. You being upset is very likely to trigger others to be upset, making a bad situation worse.

When it comes to nonverbal communications, the old adage of 'trust your instincts' is particularly true. Your subconscious will pick up on telltales and inconsistencies well before you become consciously aware of them. If you get the sense that someone isn't being honest or that something isn't consistent, you are probably picking up on a mismatch between verbal and nonverbal cues.

Some particular nonverbal cues

When I ask a group what the most honest part of the body is, most people respond with "the eyes" or perhaps "the hands". It may come as a surprise to you to know that the most honest parts of the body for most people are the feet. We learn to manage our hand gestures when we are with others, even if only to avoid knocking over our coffee cup, and we are trained from an early age to use our eyes consciously. Have you ever heard an adult tell a child to "look at me when you are speaking" or conversely been told that "dishonest people can't look you in the eye when they speak to your"? Many, if not most, liars will look you directly in the eye when they lie to you and for two good reasons. Firstly because they too have been told that being unable to look someone in the eye is a sign of dishonesty, but more importantly, they will hold eye contact for a long time because they want to know if you believe them. They are typically looking you in the eye not because they think it will help them be believable, but because they want constant feedback regarding whether what they are saying is being believed.

The most honest part of the body is actually the feet and that is because we aren't consciously aware of trying to mask them. The emotional brain however, knows when it wants out of a situation. Rather than take my word for it, I suggest you just start watching people's feet when they are in groups. The feet will point towards the person(s) that each individual is most interested in, and likewise, towards the door when they have had enough and want to leave. Next time you are in a meeting with someone and you see their feet starting to get closer to the door, or at least pointing towards it, you have used up your welcome and it's time to end the meeting. Likewise when you are chatting to someone you are interested in, when their feet are pointing towards you, you can be sure it is reciprocated. None of this is guaranteed of course and you have to look for clusters of signals to confirm people's intentions, but spend a week noticing the direction people point their feet in meetings, at parties, in the street, etc and see what you think.

Another telltale sign which can help you to see when people are uncomfortable, is touching sensitive areas. When people are uncomfortable, they will touch their neck, rub the tops of their legs under the table or otherwise touch sensitive areas of exposed skin unconsciously. We do that because stimulating the nerve endings – especially in sensitive areas such as the neck – releases endorphins in the brain to make us feel better. We don't do it in very obvious ways however. Men will adjust their shirt collar or tie, or perhaps rub the back of their neck. Women are more likely to play with or adjust jewellery such as pendants and neck chains. When you see people this, it means that they (or more correctly, the emotional part of their brains) are feeling uncomfortable.

This is just a quick overview of nonverbal communication and we've barely skimmed the surface. It's an essential topic to gain skill in if you want to be a successful and effective supervisor, friend or parent. Hopefully, I've helped develop your interest in this subject. If you'd like to know more about this subject - and I would strongly encourage you to pursue the study of nonverbal communication – I'd suggest you start with "What Every Body is Saying" by Joe Navarro and follow up with some of the 'Recommended Reading' in the Appendix of this book.

Team Meetings

"Every discussion in a meeting has a diminishing curve of interest. The longer the discussion goes on, the fewer people will be interested in it."

- Mark McCormack

Whether or not your organization calls them "toolbox meetings" or chooses another term, you need to hold regular staff meetings to ensure adequate communication. How frequently you hold them will depend on your workplace. Some organizations hold daily meetings that last about five minutes and are held standing up (a sure-fire strategy to keep them short). Other organizations might hold weekly meetings, while others decide that monthly meetings will suffice. Many managers encourage a combination of daily and weekly meetings involving different stakeholders and/or agendas. In the modern dispersed workplace, you might need to use videoconferencing, teleconferences, or webinars to get people together; fortunately, distance is no barrier to success.

Here are a handful of tips and techniques for getting the best value from your meetings, no matter where or when they're held:

> ➤ *Always* have an agenda (however informal). I refuse to go to meetings without an agenda, and you should, too.

➤ Make Health and Safety or risk management the first agenda item of *every* meeting.

➤ Appoint a chairperson. Consider rotating this role among your team members.

➤ Hold these meetings at regular times known to everyone.

➤ Pick a time when the majority of people are present (if necessary, hold two meetings on the same day to include different shifts).

➤ Circulate the minutes to people who couldn't attend.

➤ Award all of the action items to people who didn't attend. OK, this is a somewhat facetious comment (but only somewhat!).

➤ These meetings shoule be dialogue. They are the perfect opportunity for exchange of ideas and raising new issues.

Keep your get-togethers succinct and meaningful. If in doubt, remember this advice: A good meeting is a short meeting! Short, sweet, and spot-on.

Team Briefings

"Briefing is not reading. In fact it is the antithesis of reading. Briefing is terse, factual and to the point. Reading is untidy, discursive and perpetually inviting. Briefing closes down a subject, reading opens it up."

- Alan Bennett

Keep a list of the information you need to pass on and give briefings to your team at regular, specified intervals. A team briefing is:

➤ A structured formal passage of information

➤ A one-way monologue (The team can ask questions only on the material being presented.)

A team briefing is not:

➤ Ad hoc (Bring prepared notes if you want to achieve the maximum benefit in the minimum time.)

➤ A free-flowing discussion amongst the team. It's a one-way briefing with questions from the team only when needed for clarification of a particular point.

Brainstorming and Facilitation

"No idea is so outlandish that it should not be considered with a searching but at the same time steady eye."

- Winston Churchill

One of the keys to leadership is the ability to achieve work through the efforts of others. Of course, the trick isn't to simply tell them what to do. People—especially groups of people, where two heads are better than one—are smarter than most folks appreciate, so the trick is actually unleashing their full potential in a structured way. This sounds like a daunting concept to many people, so let's outline a simple process to follow. If you can master the facilitation process below, you'll soon have your team working productively and as a single entity!

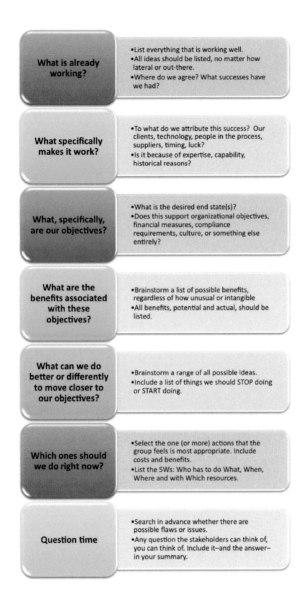

Figure 3: Facilitation process

Health, Safety, and Environment (HSE)

"There go the people. I must follow them for I am their leader."

- Alexandre Ledru-Rollin

When I first stepped into a supervisory role, the mere mention of Occupational Health and Safety (OHS, as it was called then), was enough to incite a groan and have me rolling my eyes. I'm happy to say that my views of what is now called HSE (Health, Safety, and Environment) have done a complete about-face, and I'm now an avid supporter. Ironically enough, the more training I had in OHS, the more of a fan I became.

As a supervisor, you're busy. As a first-time supervisor, you're busier than a one-armed chainsaw juggler just coming to grips with day-to-day operations. Making time to develop safety plans, conduct job hazard analyses, and prepare incident reports may seem impossible; many times, safety feels like just one more thing you have to do.

Make no mistake about it, though—responsibility for the safety and health of employees rests squarely with line management. In other words—with *you.*

This book isn't designed to replace your Workplace Health and Safety (WHS) manual or specific training. Its purpose is merely to highlight just how important WHS is to your role as a supervisor.

You may be wondering just why health, safety, and environment are often linked. The easiest way to explain that would be to say that they are essentially the same issue, stretched across different scenarios. Consider, if you will, the following examples:

➢ Safety incidents such as accidents, injuries, slips, trips, and falls have injured or killed people in hours, minutes, and even seconds. The Piper Alpha oil rig in the North Sea, for example, was destroyed by an explosion and fire on July 6, 1988, killing 167 men in a matter of mere hours.

➢ Health incidents such as bacterial infections, food poisoning, pandemics, and so forth can take days, weeks, or even longer to display symptoms and run their course. The greatest industrial disaster in Australia involved the mining of asbestos at Wittenoom, where an estimated seven hundred people have died or will die from asbestos exposure. If that's not enough, consider that an estimated one hundred thousand people in the United States have died or will die from asbestos exposure related to ship building.

➢ It typically takes years for environmental issues such as oil spills, radiation, and heavy-metal poisoning to take their full toll on human (and other) life. Chernobyl, Exxon Valdez, Bhopal, and London's Great Smog of 1952 are just a few examples of environmental incidents that have killed tens of thousands of people. One of the worst examples comes from Japan, where the dumping of mercury into Minamata Bay over a period of thirty-six years has led to the deaths of roughly two thousand people and eighty-six million dollars in payouts to more than ten thousand involved victims.

Safetymatters

HSE is one of the most critical responsibilities of a supervisor. More than a responsibility, it is an obligation to the preservation of life—human lives are on the line, and even the fate of the environment rests in your hands.

You don't need to do it all alone, however. Support and training are available on the Internet, from government agencies, in books, and through colleagues in the workplace, perhaps even from your own team. Turn to others who have HSE experience, and chances are, they will be willing and ready to assist you!

Your company most likely will have a safety contact officer or a safety adviser who will be able to point you toward the relevant safety systems you need to be familiar with. Seek them out and ask them about safety-management systems, including the following:

➢ HSE training

➢ Hazard reports

➢ Incident and near-miss reports

➢ A safety-management plan

➢ Safety bulletins

➢ Weekly housekeeping inspections

➢ Weekly safety inspections

You will certainly be responsible for the safety and welfare of all personnel who report to you and visitors, as well as for the personnel who report to your staff. Your duties may also include conducting accident investigations, closing out hazard reports, initiating workers' compensation, overseeing injury reports, and serving on a safety committee.

The most significant way you can impact HSE is to lead by example and demonstrate a visible management commitment. For example:

➢ Raise safety as an agenda item at every meeting.

➢ Support safety initiatives from within your team.

➢ Keep your eyes open for safety breaches, and act swiftly to remedy them.

➢ Encourage your team to use hazard reports.

➢ Be aware of housekeeping within your area of responsibility.

➢ Most of all, set an example—make time to do your job *safely*.

You can make a particularly strong impact via use of the housekeeping inspections and safety inspections schedule. As a supervisor, you may be responsible for ensuring that housekeeping and safety inspections are conducted as scheduled and that follow-up actions are implemented.

Time Management

"Don't say you don't have enough time. You have exactly the same number of hours per day that were given to Helen Keller, Pasteur, Michelangelo, Mother Teresa, Leonardo da Vinci, Thomas Jefferson, and Albert Einstein."

- H. Jackson Brown

As a manager and leader, your shortage of time will become as familiar to you as your best friend. It's just the reality of life; you may as well get used to it. That's not necessarily a bad thing, though. It will force you to become more productive, efficient, and effective. You'll learn just how much you can achieve. You will learn far more when the pressure is on than you ever would in the quiet times—not that there will be many quiet times.

Here are Talbot's Top Ten Tips to gain control and stay in control of your day:

1. Ruthlessly commit to starting each day by tackling your most important task.

2. Set clear goals and write them down.

3. Make it the last task of every day to prioritize your tasks for tomorrow.

4. Learn how to say no when your plate is already full.

5. Put aside time each week to improve your use of technology (e.g., learn to touch-type, watch a YouTube video on MS Excel tips).

6. Match tasks to your energy level and your most personally productive time of day (depending on whether you're a morning or afternoon person, when you're hyped up with coffee, after an exercise break, etc.).

7. Handle business-oriented paper/e-mail messages at once, if possible (and usually it is possible).

8. Restrict your e-mail to one hour per day, or keep it to a couple of specific times during the day. The best times are the hour just before lunch or just before the end of the day. That will improve your chances of finishing your work in your allotted time. Whatever you do, don't make e-mail the first task of the day—if you're like most of us, you'll just end up spending the day on it.

9. Find a way to have a four-hour block of privacy once per week to focus on a specific project.

10. Read books and listen to audio recordings on time management.

This last point is the one to take to heart above all others. The Internet is a fabulous source of information, but it's ad hoc. Formal training and education are also important, of course, but they do take a significant investment of time and money. On the other hand, books and audio recordings are cheap, accessible, and immediately useful. They can be, if you let them, the keys to your success.

Management Systems

You've probably heard the expression "management systems" used frequently in your workplace, but do you know what it means? There are all sorts of systems—environmental-management systems, quality-management systems, safety-management systems, and many, many more. Essentially, they all revolve back to the same concept. A management system is the framework of processes and procedures used to ensure that an organization can fulfill all the tasks required to achieve its objectives.

At its simplest, a management system is made up of input, a process to modify that input, output, and a feedback loop that's meant to improve the output.

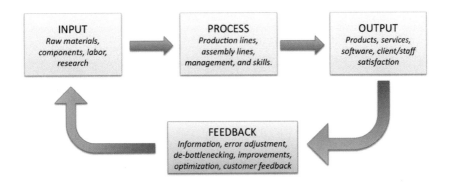

Figure 4: Basic Management System

For instance, an environmental-management system enables an organization to improve its environmental performance through a process of continuous improvement. An oversimplification of this would be "Plan, Do, Check, Act/Adjust" (PDCA), which is an iterative four-step management method used in business for the control and continuous improvement of processes and products. It is also known as the Deming Circle/Cycle/Wheel (Plan–Do–Check–Act, shown below), the Shewhart Cycle, the Control Circle/Cycle, or Plan–Do–Study–Act (PDSA).

Figure 5: Deming Quality Cycle

➤ **Plan.** As a leader, you will need to establish the objectives and processes necessary to deliver results in accordance with the expected output (the target or goals). By establishing output expectations, the completeness and accuracy of the specification also becomes a part of the targeted improvement. When possible, start on a small scale to test the possible effects.

➢ **Do.** Implement the plan, execute the process, and make the product. Collect the data you'll need for the charting and analysis in the following "check" and "act" steps.

➢ **Check.** Study the actual results (measured and collected in the "do" step above) and compare against the expected results (the targets or goals from the "plan" step) to ascertain any differences. Look for any deviation in implementation from the plan and also look for the appropriateness and completeness of the plan to enable the next ("act") phase. Charting data can make it much easier to spot trends over several PDCA cycles so that you can to convert the collected data into information. This information is what you need for the next step.

➢ **Act.** Request corrective actions on significant differences between the actual and planned results. Analyze the differences to determine their root causes. Determine where to apply changes that will ensure improvement of the process or product. When a pass through these four steps does not result in improvement, either refine the scope to which PDCA is applied so that you can plan and improve with more detail in the next iteration of the cycle or focus your attention on a different stage of the process.

A more complete system would include the element of accountability (an assignment of personal responsibility), a schedule for activities to be completed, and auditing tools to implement corrective actions, in addition to scheduled activities, creating an upward spiral of continuous improvement.

It's important to understand that there is no single model that works for every management system. Each organization and work group will need a personalized management system that suits its context, objectives, and operating style; the models provided here are just examples of potential ways to represent or implement a management system.

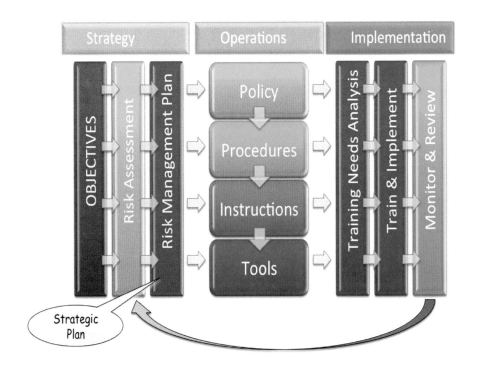

Figure 6: Example of Complex Management System

Ultimately, the purpose of a management system is simply to help an organization achieve its objectives. An occupational health and safety management system (OHSMS), for example, enables an organization to control its occupational health and safety risks and to improve its performance by means of continuous improvement.

As a short aside, it's worth mentioning that one of the reasons that two of the elements of the above graphic are devoted to training is because training is actually a fundamental but often overlooked element of management systems.

Why training? Well, training changes behavior. In turn, behavior changes attitude. And then attitude changes culture.

Figure 7: How Training Impacts Culture

As a supervisor, you are the person who has the greatest single effect on the culture of your team. There are two things you can do practically to make the greatest impact:

1. Be a role model.

2. Fight hard to get training for your people.

One of the great challenges for any manager is to create a culture that supports the organization's goals while creating a productive and simultaneously enjoyable workplace. Much has been written on organizational culture, and much more is yet to be discovered. In practical terms, your ability as a junior leader to influence organizational culture is limited. That doesn't mean that there is nothing you can do, of course. The old adage that "people don't leave a bad job—they leave a bad boss" is as true today as it ever was.

Management Policies

"Men are governed only by serving them; the rule is without exception."

- Victor Cousin

Policy is at the heart of any management system, and it provides the guiding principles for all of your day-to-day decisions.

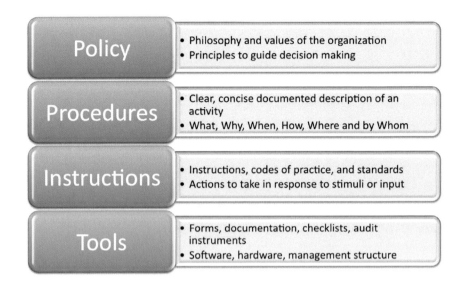

Figure 8: The Role of Policies and Procedures

When you're creating a management system, you aren't trying to run a country. Your policy needs to be only a short statement of intent. A national healthcare policy may run to fifty pages, but you should be able to say what you need to say in a single page. Make sure to address the following items:

➢ Policy

➢ Philosophy

➢ Objectives

➢ Business planning

➢ Application

➢ Performance

➢ Acceptance criteria

➢ Documentation

➢ Responsibilities

As you can see in the example policy provided in Table I, a single page is more than enough to cover all of these elements. In a nutshell, anything that states *who does what and when* is a procedure.

Table I: Example of a Management Policy

Risk-Management Policy

Policy
We are committed to a systematic and comprehensive approach to effective management of potential opportunities and adverse effects by achieving best practices in the area of risk management.

Philosophy
JBS embraces intelligent risk taking and recognizes that risk can have both positive and negative consequences.

Objectives
Risk management helps us achieve our objectives, operate effectively and efficiently, protect our people and assets, make informed decisions, and comply with applicable laws and regulations.

Business Planning
Risk management will be fully integrated with corporate processes at all levels to ensure that it is considered in the normal course of business activities.

Application

A formal risk-management strategy will be developed each year, and it will directly and demonstrably support corporate objectives. It will be implemented with the sustained involvement of all levels of the organization via adequately resourced plans with measurable timelines and objectives. Our systems will be aligned with ISO31000:2009 Risk Management Standard and supported by an ongoing program of education and training.

Performance

The success of our risk management will be measured by its impact on our corporate objectives, audits, an annual risk-management review, the ongoing collection of risk data, and the evaluation of risk models.

Acceptance Criteria

High, extreme, and/or strategic risks are controlled through senior management action with documented treatment strategies assigned. Medium risks are assigned specific management responsibility, while low risks are managed through routine procedures.

Documentation

Each stage of the risk-management process is appropriately documented, particularly where concerning the decisions and risk treatments. Individual projects and groups maintain risk registers, while enterprise risks are recorded in the strategic risk database.

Responsibilities

Risk management is a core business skill and an integral part of day-to-day activity. As individuals, we all play our part in managing risk, and staff at all levels are responsible for understanding and implementing risk-management systems in their workplace.

Managers and leaders at all levels are responsible for applying the agreed risk-management policy, guidelines, and strategies in their areas of responsibility and are expected to ensure that risk management is fully integrated with, and considered in, the normal course of activities at all levels. Visible commitment requires active participation in risk-management processes, effective resource allocation, and making risk the first agenda item at all meetings.

Divisional Managers are responsible for reporting the progress of risks and treatment plans to the Risk Management Steering Committee on a monthly basis, reporting strategic or extreme risks in a timely fashion, driving implementation of the Risk-Management Framework, and ensuring that managers are equipped with the necessary skills, guidance, and tools.

The Chief Risk Officer (CRO) is responsible for the development, coordination, and promulgation of the Risk-Management Framework, including training and systems that are capable of identifying, monitoring, and reporting documented, new, or emerging risks. The CRO is also responsible for reviewing the risk-management process and for monitoring and reporting key strategic risks. The CEO is responsible for managing risk across the organization.

Decision Making and Problem Solving

"If you're going through hell, keep going."

- Winston Churchill

You are unlikely to face the challenges that Winston Churchill confronted—but it's still safe to say that you'll not find leadership to be all plain sailing. Problem solving is one of your core responsibilities. The good news is that you are not expected to have all the answers. The bad news is that you are expected to help your team resolve virtually all the problems that come their way. Here are some of the decision-making techniques that people use in everyday life:

➤ Acquiescing to a person in authority or an expert or follow orders.

➤ Practicing consensus decision making in an attempt to avoid having "winners" and "losers." Consensus requires that a majority approves a given course of action, but the minority agrees to go along with it. In other words, if the minority opposes the course of action, consensus requires that the course of action be modified to remove any and all objectionable features.

➢ Rational decision making, also called "forcefield." This technique requires that you list the pros and cons of a potential decision and outline the advantages and disadvantages of each option. Plato and Benjamin Franklin popularized this method. It contrasts the costs and benefits of all alternatives.

➢ Calculating the opportunity cost of each option to reach a decision.

➢ Examining any and all alternatives until an acceptable one is found.

➢ Choosing the alternative with the highest probability-weighted benefit for each alternative, or simple prioritization.

➢ Employing voting methods:

- **Range voting** allows each member to score one or more of the available options. The option with the highest average is chosen. This method has experimentally been shown to produce the lowest Bayesian regret (the resulting "expected unavoidable human unhappiness") among common voting methods, even when voters are strategic.
- *Majority ruling* requires the support of more than 50 percent of the group's members. Thus, the bar for action is lower than with the rule of unanimity (consensus), and a group of "losers" is implicit.
- **Plurality,** whereby the largest block in a group decides, even if the vote falls short of a majority.

➢ Following the Delphi method, a structured communication technique for groups. It originally was developed for collaborative forecasting but also has been used for policy making.

➢ Using "dotmocracy," a facilitation method that relies on the use of special forms called Dotmocracy Sheets, which allow large groups to collectively brainstorm and reach agreement on an unlimited number of ideas they have written.

➢ Conducting a root-cause analysis. This concept takes many forms and features a variety of specialized techniques developed just for this purpose.

➤ Following the herringbone or Ishikawa diagram. Before we get to Mr. Ishikawa's legacy, however, it's worth taking a look at one of the most effective and easy-to-use problem-solving techniques that is available: the Eightfold Path of Problem Solving.

The Eightfold Path of Problem Solving

"Do not follow where the path may lead. Go instead where there is no path and leave a trail."

- Harold R. McAlindon

One of the best ways to define a scenario is to use a structured problem-solving methodology. For a small business case, you might choose to work through this as a desktop exercise or short essay. However, in most cases you are going to need a facilitated workshop with stakeholders and subject-matter experts. An example of a simple yet structured approach to scenario definition is outlined in the following eight questions:

1. What is the problem?
2. Why is it a problem?
3. What caused the problem?
4. What are the possible fixes?
5. What is the best fix (or fixes)?
6. Why is it the best fix?
7. What action must be taken to implement the best fix?
8. What are the potential flaws in this solution?

How to Use This Process

Use brainstorming and creative workshop processes to take the team members beyond their focus on a particular problem. The first step is the most important one (and typically the most time-consuming). The reason that most intractable problems appear intractable is simply because they haven't been clearly defined and agreed on. Define the problem in as few words as possible, leaving no room for misinterpretation about its meaning.

Once you've worked through the full process, you can, in many cases, implement the results immediately. In more complex situations, or when the solution is expensive, this process forms the basis of a report or business case. Simply change the headings, and your report is written. For example, change "What is the problem?" to "Background," and change "What are the possible fixes?" to "Options Considered," and so forth. Then, just like that, you've got your action plan documented.

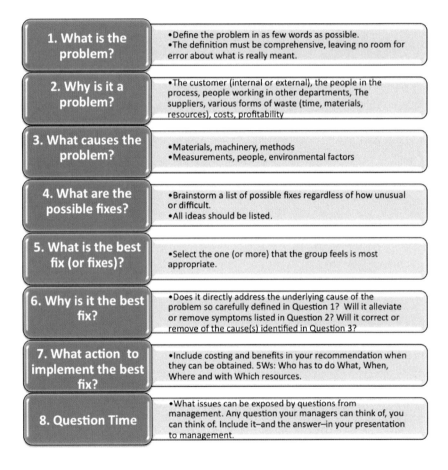

1. What is the problem?	•Define the problem in as few words as possible. •The definition must be comprehensive, leaving no room for error about what is really meant.
2. Why is it a problem?	•The customer (internal or external), the people in the process, people working in other departments, The suppliers, various forms of waste (time, materials, resources), costs, profitability
3. What causes the problem?	•Materials, machinery, methods •Measurements, people, environmental factors
4. What are the possible fixes?	•Brainstorm a list of possible fixes regardless of how unusual or difficult. •All ideas should be listed.
5. What is the best fix (or fixes)?	•Select the one (or more) that the group feels is most appropriate.
6. Why is it the best fix?	•Does it directly address the underlying cause of the problem so carefully defined in Question 1? Will it alleviate or remove symptoms listed in Question 2? Will it correct or remove of the cause(s) identified in Question 3?
7. What action to implement the best fix?	•Include costing and benefits in your recommendation when they can be obtained. 5Ws: Who has to do What, When, Where and with Which resources.
8. Question Time	•What issues can be exposed by questions from management. Any question your managers can think of, you can think of. Include it–and the answer–in your presentation to management.

Figure 9: Eight Step Problem Solving Process

1. What is the problem?

Define the problem in as few words as possible. Yet the definition must be comprehensive, leaving no room for error about what is really meant.

For example, you might (as one of my clients did) identify an issue that concerned ongoing operational losses due to cost overruns in most departments. Unfortunately, this is not a problem than can be addressed quickly. Nevertheless, from this early stage you might (with a workshop or two) eventually establish that these cost overruns occur because line managers do not receive regular profit-and-loss reports and because the reports they do receive are often inaccurate. This could be due to a number of issues and would almost certainly take volumes to fully describe, but the problem could equally (and more importantly, accurately and succinctly) be summed up as follows: "Failure to deliver organizational objectives within budget due to cost overruns as a result of inadequate financial reporting."

You might still need lengthy descriptions, graphs, or data to define the exact issues and solutions, but the ability to sum up the issue in a single, succinct statement is priceless. Let's find out how to do this consistently.

The 4 C's

The 4 C's are a handy guide to clarify your understanding of the problem:

> **Criteria**—What should be going on? What are the organizational objectives? Are we compliant with internal or external standards and guidelines?

> **Consequence**—What might happen if we do not fix the problem?

> **Condition**—What is going on?

> **Cause**—Why is this happening? What is the root cause?

Ideally, all business cases should address all four of the above elements, and the executive summary should include a sentence that sums up the 4 C's of the business case.

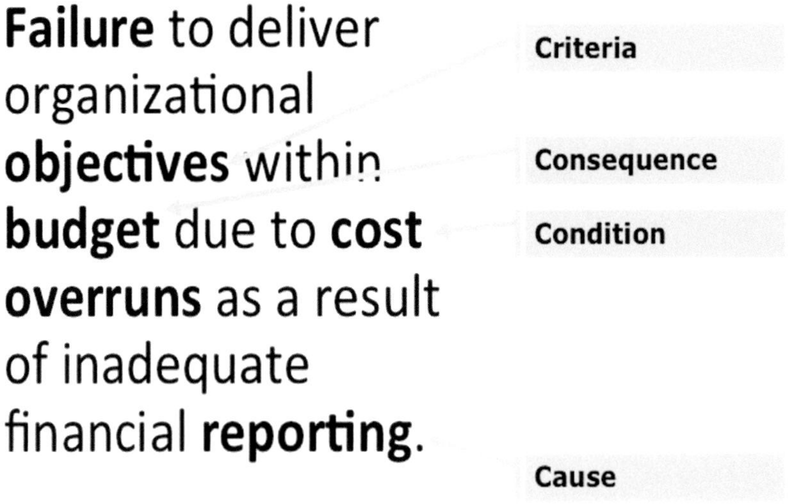

Failure to deliver organizational **objectives** within **budget** due to **cost overruns** as a result of inadequate financial **reporting**.

Criteria

Consequence

Condition

Cause

Figure 10: Example of how the 4 C's can be used in problem definition

3. Why is it a problem?

Understanding the *who* of the problem is fundamental to your business case. If you cannot clearly enunciate *why* the problem is an issue for your organization, it is probably not worthy of your (or your managers') time.

The *why* question is just a reminder that no matter how enthusiastic you are about addressing a risk, there is more at stake than just your risk assessment. Organizations exist to meet certain objectives, but that simple truth often gets lost in business-case building. Seek first to understand the impact(s) your business case is likely to have on the organization's objectives. A proposal might be a problem if it adversely affects the following:

➢ Reputation of the organisation

➢ Customers (internal or external)

➢ People involved in the process

➢ People working in other departments

➢ Suppliers

➢ Resources (time, materials)

➢ Costs

➢ Profitability

➢ Time pressures

In the example above (failure to deliver organizational objectives within budget due to cost overruns as a result of inadequate financial reporting), the potential problem is fairly obvious: Financial objectives are being threatened.

Resist the temptation to take the easy way out and just stop there; it's time now to proceed to the *cause* of the problem. In our client's case mentioned above, it turns out that the failure to meet financial objectives created an impact on a range of areas (including reputation, share price, and the viability of new projects). All of these can be fertile ground for identifying the benefits of the proposed solution. Needless to say, this situation was causing headaches for line management and also threatened individual managers' annual bonuses, so it was relatively easy to get buy-in for the processes that followed.

Keep looking further afield for the answer to *why is this a problem*, and you are going to find many more people who can help you resolve it.

3. What causes the problem?

It is not enough just to understand the risk you are planning to treat. You need to understand the underlying root cause(s). This search for the underlying catalysts must focus only on those that are within your organization's control. We are not trying to identify the root causes of terrorism or financial market instability here; we're simply trying to identify the root cause at the level that makes it an issue for the organization! The problem can spring up from a variety of sources. The following are examples of causes to get you started:

➢ Materials

➢ Resources

➢ Systems

➢ Competencies

➢ Culture

➢ Procurement

➢ Machinery

➢ Methods

➢ Measurements

➢ People

➢ Environmental factors

➢ Recruitment

The causes of the current problem will typically be complex and go back a long way, but do not overlook the obvious. Sometimes the original implementation could not afford (or did not require) the full "bells and whistles" solution. Maybe the organization did not get around to upgrading its financial reporting system because everyone was simply too busy meeting customer demands. Whatever the causes, be sure to identify them as precisely as possible.

4. What are the possible solutions?

Brainstorm *all* of the possible solutions, no matter how improbable or even impossible they seem. Discuss and shortlist possibilities until you are left with two or three of the very best solutions. Our experience (and any amount of research in the field of psychology will back this up) is that people *like* to have choices. More importantly, managers like to know that you have considered and compared a range of scenarios and options before recommending the solution at hand.

When it comes to deciding which is the best solution, there are several issues to consider:

➤ Which solution is the most effective, and why?

➤ How many issues will each solution address?

➤ What is the cost and benefit of each solution?

➤ Will this solution complement or conflict with existing initiatives and strategies?

➤ When would it become effective, and how long will it last?

There are many filters that you might apply when selecting and prioritizing potential risk solutions, but here are a few examples of the more common ones:

➤ **Your budget.** This is a common but often misguided filter. If a solution is to be truly effective, it should pay for itself with an adequate return on investment and thus warrant adding to the necessary budget. Rather than asking "What are the cheaper alternatives?" you should first ask, "How can we afford this?" Think positive, but also remember this simple adage: If you can't afford to insure the car, you can't afford the car. That's an example of the kind of thinking required. Budget is definitely important, and there is no point in having great risk solutions if they put the organization out of business. In a similar vein, if you are opening a bank in the middle of a war zone, but your budget does not cover the cost of security, it is time to either abandon that idea or find the necessary funds.

➤ **Ethics.** Personally, I dismiss any proposed risk solution that fails to pass the ethics test. This is a complex issue, but suffice it to say that any proposed solution should be consistent with the organization's values. The Ford Pinto debacle is a classic example of where this filter was not used—or, perhaps more correctly, the organization's values were inconsistent with society's values. The Pinto had design flaws to the extent that it was liable to burst into flames in a rear-impact collision. Ford's analysis, based on the number of cars in use and the probable accident rate, suggested that lawsuits due to deaths (estimated at $49.5 million) would cost less than a recall ($137.5 million). As it turned out, Ford badly misjudged this risk, was forced to do the recall anyway, and suffered measurable losses in sales associated with resulting reputation damage.

➤ **Value for money.** If a solution that costs one million dollars reduces risk by only 30 percent, but another solution can reduce risk by 25 percent for one hundred thousand dollars, which one would you choose? Your answer will depend on the organization's risk attitude, even though the second option may initially appear to be a much better bank for your buck. A similar question arises if those two risk solutions improve net income. Do they meet the organization's hurdle rate (the minimum required return on investment, or ROI)?

➤ **Effectiveness of the proposed solution.** Not all solutions are created equal. Putting a lock on a door or a "keep out" sign will probably cost a similar amount of money, but the lock is going to be far more effective.

➤ **Mutual support.** How well does the proposed solution fit in with existing measures? Multiple layers of cheap and mutually supporting solutions are usually going to be more advantageous than spending the same money on a single complex solution.

The answers to these questions depend on the context, but when it comes to the relative effectiveness of solutions, you can apply some general principles. For example, an engineering control such as handrails on a bridge above a river would be more effective than administrative controls such as putting up signs that tell people to exercise caution. Similarly, eliminating the risk of people falling into the river by moving the factory to open ground will be more effective than engineering solutions like catwalks. Note, however, that the most effective risk-reducer doesn't necessarily equate to being the most effective way of achieving organizational objectives. The cost of moving the factory is likely to be prohibitively expensive, while installing handrails is likely to be relatively inexpensive but highly effective at preventing accidental immersion in the river.

The Hierarchy of Control Concept

The Hierarchy of Control is another approach that may help you prioritize options. The following types of solutions (in order of priority) are often the most robust and effective (but not necessarily most cost-effective) solutions. The Hierarchy of Control is also known as ESIEAP due to the acronym of the steps described below:

> **Eliminate the threat** (e.g., cease the activity, stop using the toxic chemical) or eliminate barriers to the opportunity (e.g., establish a project team, review the policy, purchase the equipment).

> **Substitute a less hazardous threat** in the place of a more hazardous one, or opt for a more beneficial opportunity over a less beneficial one (e.g., use safer chemicals/processes, divest one business to purchase another).

> **Isolate the asset from the hazard** or the problem factors (e.g., Build embankments or causeways around industrial oil storage tanks, store financial data or intellectual property away from visitor areas in offices).

> **Engineer solutions** to protect the asset or modify the process (e.g., upgrade computers, employ redundant flight control systems, install airbags in cars, use automated share-market monitoring systems).

➤ **Administrative measures** to manage or mitigate the problem (e.g., train employees, employ roster/shift management, screen potential new employees).

➤ **Protective measures or personal protective equipment** (e.g., use brightly colored folders to store classified documents; secure briefcases for travel with sensitive information; use safety glasses and safe hand tools).

The concept of a "hierarchy of control" is taken from the workplace safety environment, but you can view ESIEAP as a type of onion-skin approach to choosing risk assessments. Consider, for example, how you might apply this concept to a proposed oil exploration project. In Figure 11, I have ranked six main risk solutions based on their respective effectiveness. If you see your organization as an energy company rather than as an oil company, you might consider the current potential oil prospects as being too risky and decide to eliminate that risk by focusing instead on solar energy opportunities (something that obviously won't be an option for most oil companies). There are a number of options in each of the ESIEAP circles, as illustrated in Figure 11.

Figure 11: Hierarchy of Controls example

If you filter your proposed solutions through the ESIEAP framework, you can quickly identify the most effective one. In most cases, you are going to choose an interlinked group of solutions that are mutually supportive. For example, upgrading financial reporting systems will probably require a mixture of elements. You might count primarily on an engineering fix, but the solution will also require administrative measures (like training) and some protective measures (such as using specific markings to identify reports that are not for general circulation).

5. What is the best fix?

Which of the above solutions directly addresses the problem identified above? Will you implement one or many? Similarly to the 4 C's, the quality of the business case recommendation can be judged with reference to "The 4 A's." All business case solutions should be:

➢ **Actionable**—Is it clear what must be done? When should you do it?

➢ **Achievable**—How will you know when you have done it? What are the metrics you are going to use to define success?

➢ **Appropriate**—Does it address the cause rather than the condition? Is it aligned with organizational objectives?

➢ **Agreed**—Do the authors of this business case agree with this solution? Did the people you consulted with agree? Will the stakeholders support it?

At its simplest, you should be able to summarize a business case in one sentence (or, at most, a single paragraph) in the executive summary, with reference to the 4 A's.

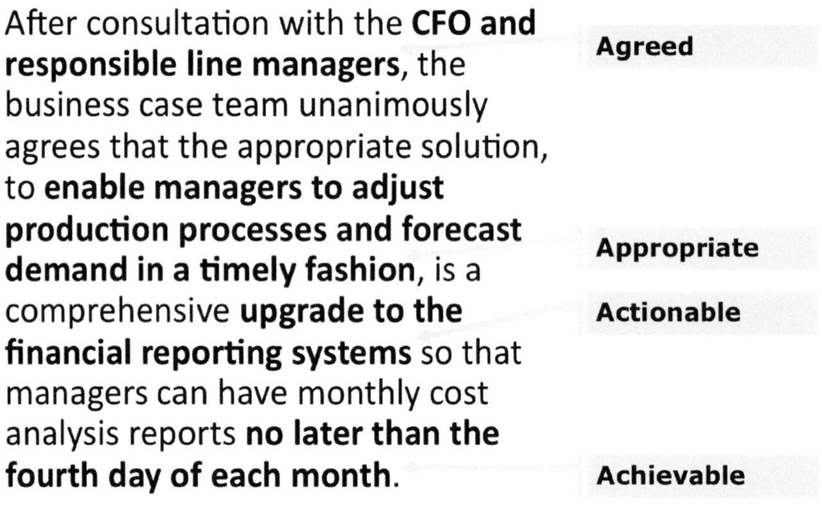

After consultation with the **CFO and responsible line managers**, the business case team unanimously agrees that the appropriate solution, to **enable managers to adjust production processes and forecast demand in a timely fashion**, is a comprehensive **upgrade to the financial reporting systems** so that managers can have monthly cost analysis reports **no later than the fourth day of each month**.

Agreed

Appropriate

Actionable

Achievable

Figure 12: Example of the 4 A's used to define a recommended solution

6. Why is it the best fix?

Does it directly address the problem so carefully defined in Question 1? Will it alleviate or remove the symptoms you listed under Question 2? Will it lead to correction or removal of the cause(s) you identified under Question 3?

7. What action must be taken to implement the best fix?

Include costing and benefits (when obtainable) in your recommendation. This is where the business case starts to come together, and, in due time, you are going to flesh this out with a project plan.

For the moment, however, focus on providing specific answers to the perennial six questions:

➤ **What**…has to be done?

➤ **Who**…has to do what?

➤ **Why**…is each phase important?

➤ **When**…does each phase happen, and how long does it take?

➤ **Where**…will things happen?

➤ **How**…will it all work?

What are the potential flaws in this solution?

Check in advance for possible flaws in your solutions before they are exposed by a question from management. Any question that your managers can think of, you can think of. Be sure to include each anticipated question and its answer(s) when presenting the solution.

Root Causes and the Ishikawa Diagram

"Shallow men believe in luck or in circumstance. Strong men believe in cause and effect."

- Ralph Waldo Emerson

Another problem-solving tool that is worth spending your time on is the herringbone, cause-and-effect, or Ishikawa diagram. It was first used by Dr. Kaoru Ishikawa of the University of Tokyo in 1943, hence its frequent reference as the

"Ishikawa diagram." You can use this diagram to identify all of the contributing root causes likely to be causing a problem or as a post-incident analysis tool. You can use this methodology on any type of problem, and you can tailor it to fit the circumstances. It has a number of key benefits:

➢ It is straightforward and easy to learn.

➢ It is a powerful visual tool for summarizing and presenting issues to management.

➢ It involves the whole team in problem identification and solving.

➢ It keeps the discussion focused on the current issues.

➢ It promotes "system thinking" through visual linkages.

➢ It prioritizes further analysis and corrective actions.

We usually use a fishbone diagram when we are trying to dig to the root cause of a problem, which may have many possible causes. It can be a useful tool to use as part of the Eightfold Path of Problem Solving, shown earlier, to help define quality problems in a format that is easily understood.

Creating this diagram gives us a pictogram of a chosen issue, along with its potential root causes. It is best constructed with a group of up to ten people. All you need is a pen, a ruler, and a large surface to write on, although having the right software is also convenient. There are dedicated software packages that conduct root-cause analysis, but you also can create them easily in any of the standard office software applications such as Microsoft PowerPoint.

The first thing you need do is to draw a horizontal line in the center of the page. At the end of the line on the far right, draw a box and write within it the effect or problem you want to investigate. Then draw a few angled lines leading into the "backbone" of the herring (voilà, this is the spine!). You can then brainstorm some main root causes and add them to the end of each angled line. It should start to resemble a fishbone.

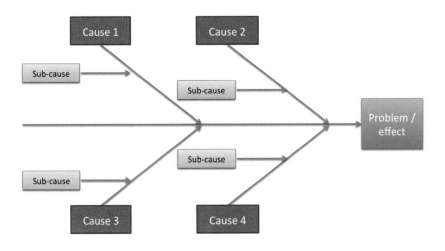

Figure 13: Basic herringbone concept

Sometimes it can be useful to pre-determine the headings you'll be putting at the end of each branch, but ideally you will probably create them from scratch for each particular problem. Either way, here are a few ideas to get you started:

> ➤ In a manufacturing situation, you can use the 6 M's as branch headings to get you started: Machines, Methods, Materials, Measurement, Man, and Mother Nature (the environment).

> ➤ In an office environment, you might use the 8 P's: Price, Promotion, People, Processes, Place, Policies, Procedures, and Product.

> ➤ Sometimes, you'll find the 4 S's to be most convenient: Surroundings, Suppliers, Systems, and Skills.

The fishbone diagram is a quick and easy tool that can help you identify root causes to even quite difficult problems. It's a great way of collating group input in a pictorial format that everyone can understand.

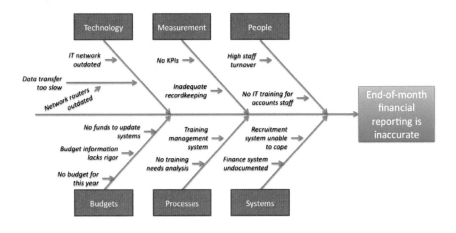

Figure 14: Complex herringbone example

Performance Management

"The beatings will continue until morale improves."

- Author unknown

Motivation

"Of course motivation is not permanent. But then, neither is bathing; but it is something you should do on a regular basis."

- Zig Ziglar

Motivation can be incredibly subtle or complex. It can be described as the psychological feature that arouses someone to take action toward a desired goal and elicits, controls, and sustains certain behaviors. At its essence, however, it derives from a basic need to minimize pain and maximize pleasure.

Volumes have been written about how to motivate employees. This isn't the place to repeat that information, so I'm going to suggest a few key concepts that will provide you with the best overall result. When trying to motivate your team members, make sure your communications have the following attributes:

➢ **Transparent.** Publish whatever performance criteria you have well in advance and let your staff comment on them.

➢ **Fair.** Be fair and equitable, but perhaps even more important, be viewed as fair.

➢ **Appropriate.** Ensure that you measure performance according to behaviors that actually reflect operational requirements, not personal beliefs or values.

➢ **Written.** Your team members are likely to consider written communications more seriously than any verbal comments you make.

➢ **Frequent.** The more frequently you sit down with staff to provide feedback, the fewer problems you'll have in the long term. Remember, what gets measured gets managed. If you *measure* people's performance, they will *manage* their own performance.

➢ **Individual.** Group performance is important and useful, but it's much more important to evaluate performance at the individual level and provide individual feedback.

Intrinsic and Extrinsic Motivation

"Motivation is everything. You can do the work of two people, but you can't be two people. Instead, you have to inspire the next guy down the line and get him to inspire his people."

- Lee Iacocca

Staff at all levels need something to keep them working. Most of the time, the salary is enough to keep employees working for an organization. If no motivation is present, then the quality of work will deteriorate.

There are essentially two kinds of motivation—*intrinsic* motivation, which comes from internal sources (e.g., "I want to do a good job"; "I want to be the fastest bricklayer") and *extrinsic* motivation, which comes from external sources ("If I don't do this in time, I'll get fired"; "If I do this well, I'll get a promotion").

Intrinsic motivation is the one you want to use with your team. It refers to motivation that is driven by an interest or enjoyment in the task itself, and it exists within the individual rather than relying on any external pressure. It's based on taking pleasure in an activity rather than working toward an external reward. People who are intrinsically motivated are more likely to engage in a task willingly and work to improve their skills, which will increase their capabilities.

Extrinsic motivation refers to the performance of an activity to attain an outcome, which contradicts intrinsic motivation. Extrinsic motivation comes from outside the individual. Common extrinsic motivations are rewards like money, grades, and threat of punishment. Research has indicated that extrinsic rewards can lead to overjustification and a subsequent reduction in intrinsic motivation.

Without overcomplicating things, the way to get the best out of your team is to understand their values—what makes them happy, why they go to work, what they enjoy. Once people have achieved a certain level of financial comfort, pay is only a small part of what they want from work. Everyone is different, so I can't give you a cookie-cutter approach other than this: Find out what motivates each and every individual member of your team, and find a way to meet their personal needs and values. Sometimes you will need to use extrinsic motivation and positive motivation (the carrot) such as pay raises and peer respect. All work well. The difficult task for most of us is counseling poor performance (the stick), and that's the topic for the next section.

Counseling and Discipline

"The trouble with most of us is that we would rather be ruined by praise than saved by criticism."

- Norman Vincent Peale

One of the most challenging yet important jobs you can perform as a "boss" is that of counseling or disciplining an employee. It is an unpleasant task that invites procrastination, yet it is essential that you react in a timely fashion to any breach of orders or poor performance.

People will work to the standard that you set, and they will perceive that standard based on the standards you accept and how you respond to discipline issues. If your responses are fair and timely, you will win their support and reinforce the best possible standards. If you let issues of discipline go unaddressed, however, you allow the poor performers to set the de facto standard for behavior on-site, and consequently you let down the rest of the team. Perhaps worst of all, the nonperforming individuals may never know they need improvement.

I remember giving a final written warning to one staff member and having him burst into tears as he exclaimed, "But I've got a wife and baby to feed!" I had a lot of compassion for him and told him as much, but I was also obliged to remind him that providing for his family was his responsibility, not mine.

My responsibility was to the other thirty staff members who were working hard and doing the right thing. I explained that if I let his poor behavior go unaddressed, I was putting the jobs of everyone at risk, and I told him I wasn't prepared or willing to do that. Once he understood my point of view—and the fact that the power to keep his job was entirely within his hands—we worked out a training, mentoring, and improvement program to get him back on track. It's important to be flexible and compassionate—but it is just as essential to be clear about your responsibilities to your team as a whole rather than toward any sole individual.

Your company's procedures manual should provide you with specific company guidelines and forms you should use for the conduct of disciplinary activities. It is not the intent of this booklet to duplicate those procedures; rather, the point is to provide you with an overview and some help in conducting disciplinary functions.

General Notes

"You are not only responsible for what you say, but also for what you do not say."

- Martin Luther

You must deal with mistakes and errors as quickly as possible. If the errors are part of the public record, then your responses should be public as well. Where appropriate, you should take responsibility for your role or contribution in the error. Do not point to a supporter or employee and say, "It was all his fault" if you were the person who hired that individual. If you do, your career as a leader will be short indeed!

With the exception of gross misconduct such as theft which warrants instant dismissal, you should deal with most issues of poor performance (e.g., failure to comply with policies) informally. Each jurisdiction will have unique legislation, and most organisations will have internal procedures. In the case of continual poor performance however, the following escalation procedure is a good general approach:

1. Informal discussion
2. Formal counseling interview and letter
3. First warning/initial formal disciplinary interview and letter
4. Second warning/second and final disciplinary interview and letter
5. Dismissal (as a last resort)

When planning a disciplinary action, follow these guidelines:

➢ Seek the advice of your supervisor before taking action.

➢ Check the company procedures manual.

➢ Discipline only when necessary.

➢ Learn the facts of the case.

➢ Check your own motivations.

➢ Schedule the interview.

➢ Arrange for an impartial witness to be present.

➢ Arrange for privacy.

➢ Keep your purposes educational.

➢ Reinforce yourself mentally.

Witnesses

Whenever a formal counseling or discipline interview takes place, it is essential to have an independent witness present. I can't emphasize this point enough! I found out the hard way when I thought it would be kinder to have an informal one-on-one chat with a staff member who was underperforming. I found out the next day that within five minutes of leaving my office, this individual was threatening to charge me with harassment. I'm happy to say that nothing came of it, and that person was simply letting off steam to colleagues rather than admitting to a lack of performance. It cost me a few stressful days nevertheless, and I never again held a counseling interview without a witness present.

The employee should have the right to have a witness of her own present, but you must absolutely ensure that you have your own witness. It is your witness who will sign the record of interview. The employee's witness may be another employee or, if you agree, someone from the union or even a family member.

Your witness should ideally be a company employee from a different work group than the employee being counseled. This is not always possible, but it is essential that you find someone who doesn't have to work closely with the employee who's being counseled. If necessary, hire someone for an hour from a temporary employment agency to fulfill this role impartially.

Whether there are one or two witnesses present, neither should enter into any discussion during the interview. They are there only to observe proceedings, not to participate. This last point is worth repeating for emphasis—*under no circumstances should a witness say anything other than to ask for clarification if he doesn't understand or hear something that was said.*

Having an impartial witness (or two) present protects everybody and, in my experience, significantly helps to defuse tempers and improve the professionalism of the entire proceeding.

Conducting Counseling or Discipline Interviews

"The utmost form of respect is to give sincerely of your presence."

- Mollie Marti

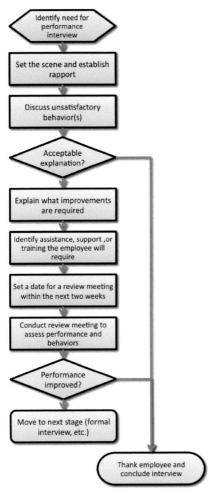

When considering counseling interviews, there is a whole school of basic approaches to counseling as an establishment of a *helping relationship*. For counseling to be effective, the process must be built on the following seven foundations:

1) People can grow and improve.
2) Counseling is an investment in the individual.
3) Counseling is a learning process.
4) Counseling can involve confrontation.
5) Acceptance of an individual as he or she is represents a good beginning.
6) Counseling is a continuous process that is likely to take more than one session.
7) The effectiveness of counseling varies with goals, but it generally is determined by some kind of change taking place.

Figure 15: Example procedure for discipline or counselling interviews

Once you have made your plans, you are ready to interact with the subordinate in the following ways:

➤ Act like a manager.

➤ Be direct.

➤ Seek information.

➤ Review the specific grievance.

➤ Look at the situation as well as the person.

➤ Separate the action/behavior from the person.

➤ Administer a reasonable penalty.

➤ Provide for some follow-up.

➤ Take notes during the interview and document the interaction.

➤ Be fair and reasonable; clearly communicate events to the team in a way that doesn't breach privacy while still providing enough information that they can see why you have taken these actions.

Informal Discussions

You must take care to ensure that even informal counseling sessions are documented and that written confirmation occurs regarding the event and outcomes. In these instances, you can keep a simple written record in a journal or diary. If the poor behavior is not addressed adequately, move on to the more formal counseling or discipline.

Discuss the details of any minor alleged unsatisfactory conduct, attitude, poor performance, or non-performance with the employee in an informal discussion. Give the employee the opportunity to respond to each allegation.

Counseling

You should use counseling in circumstances involving the following:

➢ Minor breaches by employees of their contracts of employment (e.g., minor events of absenteeism or minor discourtesies, episodic unacceptable behavior)

➢ Any performance-related issues

In very serious matters (such as serious or willful misconduct), you might need to consider immediate termination of employment. In this case, you will need to use your organization's counseling discipline procedure.

Counseling Interviews

Counseling and discipline are both about correcting behavior and addressing concerns in the workplace, but there is a huge difference between the two. It is in your power as a manager to define the situation. Some managers will look at a situation and define it in terms of a need for discipline; others will look at the same situation and define it in terms of counseling. Be sensitive to the different ramifications of these two, and give counseling a try first.

You should definitely have a witness present at this interview but be sensitive with regard to who you choose as a witness. Your witness should ideally be an employee but definitely not a peer or subordinate of the interviewee nor someone they have to work with on a daily basis.

Discipline

Discipline becomes necessary when disruptive problems must be curtailed. Some of the most common problems that warrant disciplinary actions are the non-performance of duties, chronic absenteeism, disobedience or insubordination, disruptive relationships, the damaging of property, carelessness, and the breaking of rules. Whenever these or any other disciplinary problems are judged as being serious, you should impose discipline immediately. It is important, however, to be clear about the positive goals that are to be accomplished by disciplinary action. Bear in mind that you may interpret the goals quite differently than the one receiving the discipline.

Here are examples of such goals:

➢ To be just

➢ To restore the person's behavior within the organization's discipline guidelines

➢ To protect proper procedures

➢ To deter others from making the same violation

➢ To protect employees

➢ To fulfill your role as a manager

It can be challenging to find the right balance but it is essential to allow natural justice to not only occur, but to be seen to occur. If your behavior is judged by the rest of your team to be unjust, you will undermine not only morale, but your own authority. If you are seen to be just at all times, and in all dealings, then your team will support your decisions and behavior.

Discipline Interviews

Because people are not always receptive to discipline, you should be prepared to cope with tension, hostility, anger, and disagreement. Consider potential issues such as silent hostility, open hostility, reactions to disciplining in front of others or to disciplining more than one person at a time, tears, and strained post-disciplinary relationships.

First Formal Interview

If a situation is sufficiently serious, bypass the informal discussions and begin the counseling procedure with the first formal interview.

➢ Have a witness attend this interview.

➢ Advise the employee that a support person may accompany her to the interview. This support person might be a family member, a lawyer, or a work colleague.

At this meeting, provide the employee with written details of the alleged unsatisfactory conduct, attitude, poor performance, or non-performance, and then give her the opportunity to respond to the allegations. If an informal interview has taken place, make reference to the content of that meeting.

Second Formal Interview

➢ Have a witness attend this interview.

➢ Again, advise the employee that a support person may accompany her to the interview. The support person may be a family member, a lawyer, or a work colleague.

➢ Take notes for the file.

Dismissal

As a last resort, it may be necessary to dismiss an employee after all other avenues have been exhausted. After consulting with your supervisor or human relations team, you may have to terminate an employee from their job.

➢ As in the previous two scenarios, you will need to advise the employee that a support person (family member, lawyer, or work colleague) may accompany him to the interview.
➢ Have a company witness attend the interview and take notes for the file.

A Final Thought

In many jurisdictions you won't need to follow such a rigourous process. You may even be in a location where you can legally dismiss someone without notice and it can be tempting to do so. I would however, strongly advise you to follow a rigourously fair process that provides for natural justice. Not just because it is the right thing to do but equally because if you are not only fair but are seen to be fair, you will gain the backing and support of the employees who will remain behind.

In one instance in Africa, I had a driver who was stealing fuel to sell to local villagers. I had abundant evidence based on fuel consumption, receipts and log-books that he was stealing more than he was earning in salary. It would have been tempting to dismiss him outright but I knew that I had to do it in a way that was seen by everyone (including him) to be fair and equitable. I sat with him and showed him the evidence, helped him with the math behind the fuel consumption and let him bring witnesses and supporters to the meetings. After making sure of my facts and giving him the chance to explain the multiple discrepancies he was unable to explain the missing fuel, I then gave him a letter requiring him to explain in writing the reason for the missing fuel. I also helped him find someone who spoke Swahili (his native language) but could write an articulate response in English (the official language for company business). The resulting letter didn't adequately explain why almost 800 litres (200 gallons) of diesel was unaccounted for, so I responded with a 'show cause' letter. In essence, the letter acknowledged his response to my request for for information, replied formally to it and then asked him to 'show cause' why he should not be dismissed. He was unable to do so and was subsequently dismissed.

The whole process was a lot more complicated than it would have been if I had simply (and legally in that part of the world) dismissed him from employment. Tempting as that might have been, had I simply done so, none of the other drivers and staff would have supported my actions. By being not only fair, but being transparent, when I did finally dismiss him, everyone in the camp knew the circumstances and supported my leadership for the rest of the exploration season.

Report Writing

"I love deadlines. I love the whooshing noise they make as they go by."

- Douglas Adams

Effective reports save time. They are clear, structured, and achieve their purpose. They are centered on the needs of the reader and on conveying information concisely and efficiently in plain English.

Every report should contain four basic units: the heading, the introduction, the discussion, and the conclusion/recommendations.

Heading

The heading provides a succinct summation of what the report is about.

Introduction

The introduction provides an overview of the report and outlines the terms of reference. It can include the purpose, personnel, and dates and scope. For incident reports for example, you need to document when, where, why you were called to investigate and what started the incident?

Discussion

This section summarizes the writer's activities, the problems encountered, and any other information necessary for clarity and accuracy. For incident reports, quantify what you saw and what you did to solve the problem.

Conclusion/Recommendations

This can be a summary, an evaluation of what you have learned, a statement of what decisions have been made, or any recommendations for future action. For incident reports, explain the cause of the problem. When giving recommendations, relate what could be done in the future to avoid similar problems.

At all stages of the report, ask yourself these questions:

➢ Who is going to read the report?

➢ Why am I writing the report?

➢ What do I want the reader to know/believe?

➢ How will I convince the reader?

When preparing a report, consider "4C4A" model. When writing the introduction and discussion, consider the following four C's:

➢ **Criteria**—What went wrong, and what should have happened? What criteria are you reporting against?

➢ **Condition**—What is the background or context that you observed when you started to research the report? What are the circumstances that led to the incident?

➢ **Cause**—What was the cause of the incident?

➢ **Consequence**—What was the consequence of the incident?

When presenting recommendations and the conclusion, make sure they can be described with the following four A's:

➢ **Actionable**—Are the recommendations actionable—i.e., can you actually implement them?

➢ **Agreed**—Do the stakeholders agree on the recommended course of action?

➢ **Achievable**—Can you achieve the recommended actions with the time and resources available?

➢ **Appropriate**—Are the recommendations/actions appropriate to the incident and the context?

Gaining Experience

"The only source of knowledge is experience"

- Albert Einstein

The more experience you have, the better a leader and manager you will be. Equally, the more you are paid, the more satisfaction you will gain from the role, and perhaps most significantly, the more options you will have in your career.

There are many ways you can gain experience, and not all of them are straight-forward. As many people have pointed out, the key to success is to fail faster and more often. In the words of Thomas Edison, when he was testing prototypes for the electric lightbulb "I have not failed. I've just found 10,000 ways that won't work". Rest assured, you don't need to be a dedicated genius inventor for this approach to work for you. Taking on project roles or seeking promotion is a more typical way to gain greater experience. There is however a much-over-looked avenue that can catapult your abilities and your options for promotion. The easiest way to present this concept is to relate a conversation that three of my staff members and I had some years ago. All three were applying for a promotion to a team leader's role. All were capable in most respects but lacked experience. This conversation was repeated virtually verbatim with all three of them, and it went like this:

Team member:	"I really want this promotion, and I'd like you to give me a chance at it."
Me:	"Definitely apply for it, but you know the process. At least a couple of your colleagues are also interested in the job, so it will come down to whoever is the most suitable."
Team member:	"Yes, but I'd be really good at it. The only problem is the requirement for leadership experience. It's the chicken

and the egg. How can I prove myself a good leader and get the leadership experience unless you give me a chance?"

Me: "I can see your dilemma, but I can't just take it that you'll be good at leadership if you don't have a track record or at least some experience."

Team member: "That's true, but unless you give me the job, I'll never get the experience."

Me: "Not true. Have you thought about other ways you could gain the experience?"

Team member: "Well, not really. But basically I'd have to leave to get a promotion somewhere else, or you could give me the role as an acting position."

Me: "Or you could look more laterally. How about taking up a volunteer leadership role with a local community group or perhaps joining the committee of a professional association or joining a volunteer group such as the Bush Fire Brigade Service? The Army Reserve (National Guard) also offers lots of opportunities and even pays you to undertake leadership training. I'm sure there must be something."

Team member: "Well, that's OK, but I just don't have the time. And besides, that won't help me with this promotion."

Me:	"True, time is short for all of us, but some people manage to prioritize it. Starting it now would help you with the next move. And if you'd found the time a year or two ago, you would already have a solid track record in leadership."
Team member:	"Yes, but if you'll just give me a chance, then I'll be able to gain the experience."

You can probably see where I was going with this conversation and how resistant to it my team members were. None of the three took my suggestions to take on volunteer leadership roles or even to take a leadership course, and none of them got the job. Only one of them is in a leadership position today, and that is with a different organization. Think laterally—there are any number of opportunities for you to expand your experience and abilities.

About half of my leadership experience has come from unpaid or low-paying roles. As a team leader in the Volunteer Ambulance Service and as a patrol commander in the Army Reserve, I made many mistakes but gained enormous amounts of practical experience with hands-on leadership and decision making in high-pressure situations. As a director of not-for-profit boards and professional associations, I blundered along on many occasions, but equally, I learned an enormous amount about strategic leadership and management. In all of those roles, the mentoring and networking were invaluable. I also learned a lot about myself, grew as an individual, and gave a lot back to the community.

In his inaugural address on January 20, 1961, US President John F. Kennedy said, "Ask not what your country can do for you. Ask what you can do for your country." If you keep this approach in mind, you will gain more by helping your community than you could ever anticipate.

Some Final Thoughts

"Leadership and learning are indispensable to each other."

- John F. Kennedy

After all that, you're probably wondering what you should actually do as the next step. I'm hoping that you've picked up a few ideas from this book and are inspired to go out and implement them.

One of the challenging aspects of leadership is that the buck stops with you. It's interesting how little we know about our boss's jobs until we are a manager ourselves. I remember coming back from a two-week holiday, during which one of my team leaders had been doing my job. His greeting on my return went something along the lines of "I hope you had a great holiday, but thank goodness you're back! We used to think you sat in that office and did nothing all day. Oh, how wrong we were. I'm so glad you're back. I'm exhausted."

You aren't expected to know all the answers, but ultimately you are the captain of the ship, and you are accountable for not only your actions but those of your team. It's a sobering and sometimes scary proposition, but unless you are prepared to adopt and understand that fundamental principle, you would be best advised to remain happily as a follower. For those who can accept the responsibility, leadership can be one of the most satisfying activities you will ever undertake. What you will take with you to the end of your life will be the satisfaction you get from helping others achieve their true potential—and the satisfaction of knowing that you achieved your full potential.

One of the challenges you will face along the way is communicating with people in a way that motivates them. An old boss of mine gave me some sage advice on this topic, and I'm going to share it with you. He said, "People don't judge what is important by what you say is important. Contrary to popular opinion, they don't even judge it by your actions. They judge what you believe to be important by where you spend your time. People aren't stupid. They know your time is precious, so if you choose to spend it behind a computer screen doing e-mail, then they, too, will focus on e-mail. If, however, you spend your time with them, your staff will know that they are your highest priority." In plain English, get out from behind the desk and spend your time with your people. Get to know their values and passions. Is it family, sport, hobbies, current affairs? You need to know what motivates them as a human being. Spend some time with them even if you have to use work tasks as the opportunity. Roll up your sleeves and help them when they get stuck on a task. Take the time to chat with them and find out about them. If you send your team for a day of training, that sends a powerful message that you are investing in them. But it's even more powerful if you can *open* the first session of that training. Your presence there will speak volumes about their importance to you and your perception of the skills they are about to learn.

That leads us nicely into my final thought on the topics of leadership and management. Life is a process of continuous learning, and that is especially so for leaders. This book can provide you with some insight into management and leadership, but it is just a small step. My final advice on this top is simply this: Leaders are readers!

If you can devote one hour per day to reading, you will read one book per week. In one year, you will have read 52 books, and in just five years, you will have read 260 books. That is a staggering amount of information. You can put yourself into the top 1 percent of experts on any topic in the world through this simple act. And yes, one hour per day is a challenge, but think of it as an investment. Most people spend more time watching sports or sitcoms than they do working on themselves, so perhaps the occasional sacrifice of television-watching hours will be worth it. Instead of reading a newspaper over breakfast and watching the news each evening, try reading a book. Most of the news isn't adding any value to your life, and trust me, if something really significant happens, people will tell you.

If reading doesn't appeal to you for some reason, you could try listening to podcasts, audio books, training courses, and online video training. The important thing is to be consistent. Even if you don't find an hour every day, treat it as an average and dedicate seven hours per week to your future. Your income, health, happiness, and sense of personal satisfaction will soar if you commit one hour per day. Try it for a month—it will become a habit, and I think you'll like it.

Good luck with your leadership and management career. I hope it brings you much success and personal enjoyment.

Appendix: Recommended Reading

I started out with a long list of recommended reading, but there are thousands upon thousands of great management and leadership books out there. You'll find them along your journey, and part of the fun is discovering them for yourself. I suggest that you read the following books first. Most of them are short and very easy to read. All of them will leave you with new insights. Enjoy.

The Art of War
Sun Tzu

Emotions Revealed, Second Edition: Recognizing Faces and Feelings to Improve Communication and Emotional Life
Paul Ekman

Fish! A Proven Way to Boost Morale and Improve Results
Stephen C. Lundin, Harry Paul, John Christensen, Ken Blanchard

Good to Great: Why Some Companies Make the Leap…and Others Don't
Jim Collins

How to Win Friends and Influence People
Dale Carnegie

The One Minute Manager
Ken Blanchard and Spencer Johnson

Please Understand Me II
David Keirsey

Positive Leadership: The Game Changer at Work
Steve Gladis

The Power of Less: The Fine Art of Limiting Yourself to the Essential...in Business and in Life
Leo Babauta

The 7 Habits of Highly Effective People
Stephen R. Covey

The Tipping Point: How Little Things Can Make a Big Difference
Malcolm Gladwell

What Every BODY is Saying: An Ex-FBI Agent's Guide to Speed-Reading People
Joe Navarro

What Got You Here Won't Get You There: How Successful People Become Even More Successful
Marshall Goldsmith and Mark Reiter

Who Moved My Cheese? An Amazing Way to Deal with Change in Your Work and in Your Life
Spencer Johnson with Kenneth Blanchard (Foreword)

A Corporate Tool

If you liked this book and would like to inquire about a corporate license for your intranet, volume discounts, leadership training, or customizing this book for your organization, please contact me at www.juliantalbot.com.

Made in the USA
Coppell, TX
15 February 2020